VGM Opportunities Series

OPPORTUNITIES IN HOSPITAL ADMINISTRATION CAREERS

I. Donald Snook, Jr.

Foreword by
John A. Russell
President
The Hospital Association of Pennsylvania

VGM Career Horizons
a division of *NTC Publishing Group*
Lincolnwood, Illinois USA

Cover Photo Credits:
Upper left, upper right, and lower left courtesy of International Business Machines Corporation. Unauthorized use not permitted.
Lower right courtesy of Harrisburg (Pa.) Hospital. Reprinted by permission of Sherry Migliore.

Library of Congress Cataloging-in-Publication Data
Snook, I. Donald.
    Opportunities in hospital administration careers / I. Donald
Snook, Jr.
        p.   cm. — (VGM opportunities series)
    Previously published in 1988.
    Includes bibliographical references.
    ISBN 0-8442-4562-3 (alk. paper). — ISBN 0-8442-4563-1 (pbk. :
alk. paper)
    1. Hospitals—Administration—Vocational guidance.   2. Hospitals—
Administration—Vocational guidance—United States.   I. Title.
II. Series.
RA971.S66   1997
362.11'068—dc21
                                                        96-40277
                                                        CIP

3 6626 10152 742 2

Published by VGM Career Horizons, a division of NTC Publishing Group
4255 West Touhy Avenue
Lincolnwood (Chicago), Illinois 60646-1975, U.S.A.
© 1997 by NTC Publishing Group. All rights reserved.
No part of this book may be reproduced, stored in a retrieval
system, or transmitted in any form or by any means,
electronic, mechanical, photocopying, recording or otherwise,
without the prior permission of NTC Publishing Group.
Manufactured in the United States of America.

7 8 9 0 VP 9 8 7 6 5 4 3 2 1

CONTENTS

Brief history of hospitals. The modern era. Evolution of health administration.

Administrative roles. The administrator as leader. Health administration as a profession. Inside hospital activities. Outside hospital activities.

The medical care system. Outreach component. Outpatient component. Inpatient component. Extended component. Community at large component.

Types of hospitals. Hiring the chief executive officer (CEO). Senior administrative staff. Job summaries and compensation.

Administrators in finance. Administrators in support services. Administrators in nursing. Administrators in planning and marketing.

ABOUT THE AUTHOR

I. Donald Snook, Jr., is a nationally renowned leader in hospital management and marketing and is president of Presbyterian Foundation for Philadelphia. Prior to assuming this position, he was CEO of Presbyterian Medical Center of Philadelphia.

Mr. Snook has contributed numerous articles to health care management literature and is the author of several books, including the widely read *Hospitals: What They Are and How They Work*. He is the originator of the "hotel-hospital" concept. He is the recipient of the American Healthcare Marketing Association's "CEO Marketer of the Year" award and received the Senior Regent award from the ACHE, Southeastern Pennsylvania region.

Mr. Snook holds a B.B.A. in marketing from the Wharton School of the University of Pennsylvania (cum laude), and an M.B.A. in hospital administration from George Washington University. He has also completed the Health Management Systems Program at the Harvard Business School.

Mr. Snook is a faculty member in the graduate program in health care administration at LaSalle University and Pennsylvania State University. He is a fellow in the American College of Healthcare Executives. Mr. Snook has conducted seminars nationally on contemporary issues.

FOREWORD

Careers in hospital administration offer exciting challenges and opportunities. The work is important, demanding, and personally rewarding. You work with dedicated and talented people in providing vital human services. You deal with complex management, financial, and social problems. Hospitals function at the center of our nation's health care system, and individuals who want to assume leadership responsibilities in creating the well-managed community hospitals of tomorrow will find very rewarding careers.

Don Snook has prepared an excellent book to assist you in choosing a career in hospital administration. He points out that collectively, hospitals are one of our nation's largest employers and offer many career options. Don is recognized as an articulate spokesperson and advocate for our industry, and this book is written out of his experience in counseling many people about opportunities in health careers.

The book points out that the health field, especially in the past decade, has experienced tremendous growth and that jobs in health administration are exciting but also call for a great deal of knowledge, stamina, and patience. People who succeed in hospital administration combine excellent people skills with management skills. The critical challenge is to ensure that patients receive high quality health care, in the most appropriate setting, within the resources available.

It is my privilege to work with health care executives from Pennsylvania and throughout the United States, and in general I find them to be very able executives who have a strong commitment to public service by providing health care services to their communities.

I hope readers of this book will be motivated to further explore the varied and expanding opportunities in hospital administration careers and join us in our important work.

> John A. Russell
> President
> The Hospital Association of Pennsylvania

INTRODUCTION

BRIEF HISTORY OF HOSPITALS

Today's health care industry is one of the largest businesses in the country. It is a system that has grown in size and technology as well as in quality. Its historical roots were relatively modest, starting in precolonial times with a few primitive health care institutions primarily to serve the poor. The first recorded American health care institution was the almshouse established on Manhattan Island in 1663 to care for sick soldiers and sailors. A model for today's voluntary community hospital was launched in 1751, when in Philadelphia Benjamin Franklin started the Pennsylvania Hospital. America's first Catholic hospital was started by the Daughters of Charity of St. Vincent DePaul in St. Louis, Missouri, in 1828. It was called the DePaul's Hospital. It was not until the latter part of the nineteenth century, following the work of Louis Pasteur in bacteriology and Joseph Lister in antiseptic surgery, that the hospital began to take on the image of a place to get well, not a place to die. Following that, the introduction of sulfa drugs in the mid-1930s and the use of penicillin in the 1940s made surgery safer by lessening the chance of mortality due to infection.

THE MODERN ERA

After World War II medical technology grew rapidly. With the first successful kidney transplant in 1954, medicine entered the era of "spare parts." Hospitals have always been and continue to be part of this technological revolution in prosthetic devices such as artificial hearts and blood vessels.

In 1966, with the passage of the Medicare and Medicaid legislation, hospitals embarked upon a partnership with the federal government. Since that time the growth of the government's involvement in the hospital and health care business has been dramatic. It is common for health care institutions to have to deal with dozens of regulatory governmental agencies. Working with these agencies is one of the constant challenges for the modern health administrator. The American hospital as an institution has been dynamic and exists today as the mother of many other health institutions because it has met the needs of the people. Hospitals and health care institutions are still writing their history as they continue to evolve to meet society's changing needs and to improve the technology of health care and health care delivery.

Scarcely any other field or industry in the United States is changing more rapidly than the nation's health care system. The innovative ways in which health care is financed and delivered today are bringing radical changes.

Over the last several years, merger mania has been sweeping the U.S. health care industry, realigning relationships among physicians, hospitals, and managed care organizations in markets large and small. Hospitals are continuing to merge and consolidate, the integration of health care systems is evolving, hospital bed capacity and occupancy continue to decline, and the volume of outpatient services is rising. Investments in information systems—both administrative and clinical—are expanding, along with efforts to document treatment outcomes. Greater emphasis is being placed on patient satisfaction and how it is measured.

EVOLUTION OF HEALTH ADMINISTRATION

Health administration in general, and hospital administration in particular, engage in much the same activities that most commercial enterprises do. In the health administration business, however, the administrative and service functions found commonly in commercial enterprises are integrated with a host of additional complex activities—for example, laundry, power plant engineering, dietary service, maintenance, and a variety of technical nursing and medical care activities. This makes hospital administration a challenging, innovative, and demanding profession. The hospital or health care administrator must be concerned with people, programs and services, and facilities and equipment.

Just as our health care system has become more complex, so has the role of the key decision maker, the health service administrator. Health care institutions have become more specialized and more sophisticated, and accordingly, so has the administrator's role. At one time hospital administrators were taken from the ranks of the nursing department; in church-related hospitals, it was common for the administrator to come from the religious order or perhaps from the retired clergy. It was also a common practice to promote the hospital's business manager or accountant to the chief administrator's job, or even to recruit a retired businessman or a retired physician to assume the position of administrator. Those days have passed.

Today the health care administrator must have a broad base of skills and scientific knowledge integrated with business and humanistic talents. Being able to work with people and show diplomacy, creativity, and flexibility is essential for modern health care administrators. It is absolutely necessary for them to have these skills if they are going to guide and coordinate all the diverse elements of modern health care organizations.

As far back as 1929, Michael M. Davis, Ph.D., recognized this in his book *Hospital Administration: A Career.* When the first graduate program in hospital administration was established in 1934 at the University of Chicago, it was quite appropriate that Dr. Davis was appointed its director. Yet roots of professional management in hospitals go back further than the first formal university training program. In 1898, certain administrators of hospitals in the United States and Canada formed a professional group known as the Association of Hospital Superintendents of the United States and Canada. The formation of this group was the earliest recognition of hospital administration as a separate profession. This group was later to become the American Hospital Association, whose membership today includes most hospitals in the United States. Later still, in 1933, leading administrators from this country and Canada organized the American College of Hospital Administrators, and in 1985, changed its name to the American College of Healthcare Executives (ACHE) to more properly reflect the changing role and nature of hospital management, which today helps give direction and recognition to the hospital and health care administration profession.

CHAPTER 1

WHAT IS HEALTH ADMINISTRATION?

Hospital and its broader term, health administration, is really the central component in the management of health institutions and agencies. People engaged in management of health services are recognized as professionals under the umbrella of health services administration, including its major component, hospital administration. *Health administration* is a broad term. It encompasses various management activities, including planning, organizing, controlling, and supervising, as well as evaluating institutional and community resources, systems, and procedures by which the needs and demands of the health and medical care systems are met.

As new political, economic, and social policies began to focus on health care in the mid-1960s, greater demands were placed on health care managers. Some of the factors influencing the management of health care services include the enormous pressure for specific performance, new events in the health care environment, and technological advancements. Even today, these factors continue to affect the health care industry.

Management is directing various functions in an institution to help make a health organization work. Administrators do this personally in smaller operations and by working through a staff of assistants in larger institutions.

Health administrators are called upon to make many decisions; for example, they may approve budgets and negotiate contracts. Assistant hospital administrators may direct the daily operations of various departments, such as the food service, housekeeping, and maintenance departments.

More specifically, hospital administrators, whether they are employed at a large urban hospital or a small rural facility, are responsible for managing the entire hospital operations and all its related units. The administrator is hired by the board of trustees, the hospital's governing authority, and is responsible for seeing that the board's policies are carried out.

ADMINISTRATIVE ROLES

Administrators assume various roles while managing their institutions, but most administrators fit into at least one, and sometimes all, of three specific roles. They are either a business manager, an institutional coordinator, or a chief executive. To some degree, most administrators assume some part in all of these roles. In the business manager role, the administrator is responsible for many of the institution's internal operations. This means that he or she must order and procure supplies, manage personnel, and provide physicians and other health care professionals with the resources they need to do their job.

In the role of business manager, the administrator is concerned with financial and statistical data—the basic reports of the hospital's financial affairs. The visitor to the hospital may find the administrator pouring over computer printouts or working with columnar pads and calculators. This side of an administrator's work uses his or her ability to understand statistics and finance.

As a coordinator, the administrator has to develop more of an outside role. In this role the administrator becomes influential as a negotiator, particularly with insurance plans that pay patients' hospital bills. Being active in public relations is also part of the coordinator's role. In this capacity administrators work with very diverse groups. They may be seen in the physician's lounge having coffee and chatting about a problem on the medical staff or making administrative rounds and keeping in touch with employees, patients, and visitors. Perhaps the most important tool of the administrator as coordinator is communication. Communicating in writing, orally in public speaking, or over the telephone are all important in getting the job done successfully.

As the hospital's chief executive, the employees, staff, board, and public have a right to expect the administrator to look the part of an executive. This means the administrator must be well groomed and dressed appropriately. The dress style could be conservative, as it is in many institutions, or less formal, which is common in some parts of the country. The important element is that the administrator be dressed appropriately for the time and situation.

The administrator as executive has brought about some title changes to the position. The chief administrator may carry the title executive director, executive vice-president, or president and chief executive officer (CEO). As you can see from the number of titles, the definition of health administration is quite broad. It encompasses the management of many various institutions and tasks. But all institutions have one thing in common—they provide medical and health services.

THE ADMINISTRATOR AS LEADER

There is a big difference between being a manager and being a leader. The health care industry is demanding that the health care CEOs take on the role of "leader." Where management is a process impacted by the individual manager's style and experience; it is leadership that gives management its purpose and direction. In response to the question—What one characteristic is required of effective leaders? A sample of accomplished and outstanding health care executives responded:

"Good leaders must have vision of purpose. They need to know where they want to go, how they want to get there, and who they want to take with them."

—Diane M. Howard, FACHE

"As healthcare executives, we must identify the right direction for our organizations and inspire our teams to strive toward that vision."

—Captain (P) David P. Budinger, USA, CHE

"A good leader must have integrity and instill it in all areas of the organization. A leader upholds the values, ethics, and mission of the organization."

—James E. Dalton, Jr., FACHE

"Good leaders adapt and evolve without losing sight of their quest to move their organizations through enormous changes and challenges."

—Donna G. Case, FACHE

HEALTH ADMINISTRATION AS A PROFESSION

In 1939 the American Hospital Association and the American College of Hospital Administrators jointly produced a code of ethics for hospitals and administrators. This gave hospital and health administration the principles needed to grow as a profession.

The Evolution of Hospital Administration as a Profession

Hospital administration involves many of the same activities that most institutional administrators and managers are involved with. The profession of hospital administration is unique because hospitals are a complex association of professionals all working in a "life-and-death" activity. Hospitals have administrative and service functions which are common to other commercial enterprises, but they also have complex and unique services integrated with the usual departments. In a hospital you find maintenance, laundry, and power plant alongside of highly technical nursing and medical care activities. This variety and complexity is what makes hospital administration such a demanding profession. Fundamentally, hospitals are people, and hospital administrators are primarily concerned with people.

In earlier times the hospital administrator could well have been selected from the ranks of the nursing service. It was common to find registered nurses serving as institutions' head administrators. In church hospitals, particularly Catholic hospitals, it was common to select the administrator from the ranks of the religious order. These earlier administrators were diligent, hard-working, and quite competent. Many administrators also came up from the ranks of the business office. Occasionally the hospital was managed by a retired businessman. The days of this type of vertical mobility up to the CEO's rank is gone. In the mid-1930s the first formal university course for hospital administrators was offered. After World War II, the field of hospital administration gained in status as the need for formally trained hospital administrators increased. In 1933 an organization was founded, the American College of Hospital Administrators (ACHA). Most recently it has changed its name to keep pace with what is happening in the field. Its name is now the American College of Health Executives (ACHE). The College encourages the highest standards of education and ethics in the hospital administration profession. (The ACHE code of ethics specifically mentions how health administrators are to be accountable in their performance.) There are formal training programs in a number of universities throughout the United States and Canada today. These universities offer degrees in hospital administration at the baccalaureate, master's, and even doctoral level. Formal training programs for hospital administrators cover at least three general levels: (1) administrative theory, (2) medical and health care delivery, and (3) business functions, including organization and management theory.

There have been numerous indications of hospital administration's growth, including the publication of a variety of well respected technical and professional journals in the field. These add to the specialized body of knowledge for the management and planning of health services. In addition, there are highly specialized professional organizations that represent the field of hospital and health administration.

The Physician as Administrator

Just as in years gone by hospital administrators may have been nurses, members of a religious order, or accountants or business office managers who worked their way up through the organization, now there is a trend for physicians to take a greater role in hospital management activities. Physicians are taking greater interest in the hospital decision-making process because it affects their professional lives. Some physicians are assuming the top, the chief executive officer's role. There are also other management roles for physicians. The hospital's medical director is usually an employee who has senior administrative responsibilities. The chief of the medical staff is another administrative physician whose responsibility is to coordinate the functions of the medical staff. This position provides an excellent training ground for learning supervision of personnel and resources. Many larger hospitals have full-time department heads, the chief of medicine, and the chief of surgery. All of these are excellent opportunities for physicians who wish to move up into the CEO ranks. It is likely that in the future more physicians will seek executive management jobs.

INSIDE HOSPITAL ACTIVITIES

Historically, the hospital administrator's job was just to manage those things that went on in a hospital. Part of the job was to oversee all the buildings, grounds, and facilities and to see that these were in proper order and that the hospital's personnel were qualified and performed their jobs well. It was the administrator who had to answer legally for the acts of his or her employees under the principle of *respondeat superior.*

Maintaining a positive relationship and effective communication with the hospital's physicians is a key internal duty. An effective administrator has to be a competent communicator. Remember, the administrator is the board of trustee's agent, and, as such, may have to monitor medical ethics and morals, as well as the hospital's rules and regulations.

Dealing with People

The administrator deals with many different kinds of people and groups. But there are several groups of individuals that the administrator must deal with regularly in the course of a day. Effectively working with these groups allows the administrator to operate the institution more efficiently. Some of the groups include the administrator's first-line supervisors, the institution's board of trustees, the medical staff, the employees, patients, the public, hospital vendors, other health administrators, and governmental and other regulatory agencies.

Dealing with the Board of Trustees

The board of trustees is the governing body of the institution, and gives the administrator his or her ultimate authority. In other words, the board is the administrator's boss. It delegates to the administrator the authority to manage the affairs of the hospital or institution. The official relationship is that of an employer and employee, but actually the administrator and the board function more as partners. The administrator is the representative of the board in the daily activities of the institution and should at all times be dignified and professional. As the administrator, you will attend board committee meetings as well as meetings with medical staff. Administrators make formal reports and recommendations to the board of trustees regarding the hospital's activities.

In some institutions the administrator, by virtue of the position itself, may also be a member of the board. Boards have to be directly accountable to the community and to the public served by their hospital or institution. Over the last several years, boards have been reviewing more frequently management's decisions to make sure that they are in compliance with board-developed policies. Some of the real challenges for both the administrator and the board arise when they and the institution fall under the scrutiny of the mass media. And perhaps the most important task before the board and administration is working together to continually improve the institution's quality of care.

Dealing with the Medical Staff

The administrator acts in partnership not only with the board of trustees, but also with the physicians and other health care personnel. Under the best circumstances, the administrator has a mutual understanding with, respect for, and trust in the members of the medical staff. One of the key responsibilities of a hospital administrator is to communicate with the hospital's medical staff. It is the administrator's job to see that the physicians have the proper tools in the right place at the right time in order for them to carry out their role in the hospital.

Successful administrators must be effective in keeping their medical staff informed about organizational changes, board policies, and decisions that affect them and their patients. Hospital medical staffs, though answerable to the board and its management ultimately, are also self-governing and have their own bylaws. The administrator should be sensitive to the medical staff's needs for self-governance and support that need. From time to time natural frustrations will arise between the medical staff and the administration. Frequently the sources of this conflict can be attributed to poor communication. Administrators must communicate effectively with the medical staff if the hospital is to function efficiently. Consequently, the administrator must always be available to medical personnel for consultation.

Dealing with Employees

It is the employees that provide the working force for the hospital. This group possesses a variety of personalities, educational backgrounds, and expertise. The employee group provides many of the administrator's day-to-day challenges. Personnel raise many complex human problems for the administrator. The employees must look to the administrator as their work leader. It is the administrator's role to keep the employees informed of the critical role their services play in the successful operation of the hospital or institution. This is easier to achieve with nurses and others who deliver direct patient care, but the administrator must continually be informing all employees of their mission and importance. In dealing with employees at all levels, it is critical that the administrator show objectivity, understanding, and fairness. The administrator must handle the authority to employ, direct, discipline, and dismiss employees with these important principles in mind.

Dealing with Patients and their Families

The administrator has a vital role in public relations when meeting with patients and their families. He or she must fulfill all their legitimate requests for general comfort and care in order to assist their recovery. In dealing with patients the administrator must also understand the patient's visitors and relatives. It is important that the administrator safeguard confidential patient information just as doctors and nurses do. Confidential information, whether from patient or staff, belongs to the institution and must not be used by administrators or others for their own gain or self-interest. In fact, no hospital insiders should use a patient's information improperly. Misuse of this material or knowledge is also a violation of the code of ethics of ACHE.

OUTSIDE HOSPITAL ACTIVITIES

There are a host of outside responsibilities facing administrators. They must understand and participate in appropriate community activities. Staying in touch with the latest government rules and regulations is essential to the well-being of the institution. Maintaining government relations is important to the administrator. There is often a need to maintain a social presence in the community. Administrative growth can be developed by participating in continuing education activities. The hospital administrator is the board's agent, and the board of trustees is accountable to the community; therefore, finding out what is going on in the marketplace and bringing these new changes back to the hospital is important. The CEO is expected to show leadership within the hospital and outside its walls. The administrator has a major role in educating the community on hospital matters. This is particularly important as consumers clamor about rising hospital costs. The public relations department can be an important ally for the administrator in reaching the community. Publishing brochures and pamphlets and participating on radio and TV shows to spread the hospital's message is becoming a familiar task for administrators.

With the passage of Medicare in 1966, hospitals and government became intertwined. Today's administrator must stay on top of the latest government rules and regulations concerning funding, reimbursement, and planning issues. Administrators meet with governmental reimbursement agencies, planning bodies, and politicians in order to keep up-to-date. Hospitals need a master or strategic plan. This type of planning takes a great deal of effort and time. The administrator may work with regional planning agencies and community groups to draft the institution's plan.

Dealing with the Public

It is the administrator's job to remain in close contact with the community that sponsors the hospital or health care institution. The administrator has the responsibility to foster favorable public relations in the community. The administrator is responsible for maintaining the institution's positive image among the community's residents. To this end, the administrator may initiate community activities, such as health fairs and health screening programs for the public. Other public contact may be achieved through public speaking engagements, or by releasing information to the press, or by broadcasting over radio and television. The administrator must realize that the institution has a responsibility to the public and that the public has a right to be informed. The administrator is important in this process. How successful he or she is in this role to a large extent determines the reputation of the hospital. One way the administrator can establish effective communications with the public is by staying in personal contact with key members of the community, and keeping them up to date on all matters regarding the institution's policies.

CHAPTER 2

WHERE ADMINISTRATORS WORK

THE MEDICAL CARE SYSTEM

Administrators work in the health service and medical care systems in this country. Webster defines a *system* as a set or arrangement of things so related or connected as to form a unity or organic whole. More specifically, the health system or medical care system is a set of mechanisms through which human resources, health care facilities, and medical technology are organized by means of administrative structures. The medical care system offers integrated services in sufficient quantity and quality to meet the community's demands at a cost compatible with the community's financial resources. It is within this medical care system that administrators find jobs. The American medical care system has five distinct elements. Four of these elements or components are related to specific institutions; the fifth element encompasses or surrounds these institutions and is called the community at large. Let us examine each of the components and institutions with which the medical care system is associated and specifically highlight the institutions and agencies in which administrators work and are needed.

OUTREACH COMPONENT

Perhaps the best place to start our review of the medical care system is with the outreach component. It is a general rule of thumb in this country that the traditional medical care system attempts to meet the primary medical care needs of its patients through outreach programs. These programs are generally decentralized and widely scattered. One of the earliest and most common type of outreach services is solo medical practitioners with offices located in neighborhoods. Physicians with private practices provide the bulk of care to the middle class in this country, but the urban poor continue to use city health clinics and similar institutions as a substitute for family physicians. Other forms of the outreach component include neighborhood community health centers, community mental health agencies, physician group practices, and a variety of other ambulatory care arrangements including the outreach activities of health maintenance organizations (HMOs).

Hospitals also have reached out into their communities and demonstrated a new emphasis on preventive care by adding or expanding health promotion services. These educational and support services are intended to help individuals learn how to reduce their health risks, manage their health, and use health services effectively. They may be targeted at patients, through patient education services, or at residents of the community who are not currently patients.

OUTPATIENT COMPONENT

Another area of our medical care system is outpatient care. One of the major institutions providing this component is the traditional hospital clinic. The growing outpatient services also includes emergency facilities. Large numbers of patients continue to use emergency rooms steadily across this country. Also included in the outpatient component are ambulance squads, whether they are community, municipal, or police or fireman rescue squads. Ambulance assistance is an outpatient service that has taken on increased status with the advent of paramedics, emergency medical technicians (EMTs), and emergency medical systems, such as the cardiopulmonary resuscitation teams that have saved so many lives. Physician group practices are common in larger medical centers and are also included in this outpatient category.

Even more dramatic than the decline in inpatient hospital use has been the increase in community hospital outpatient visits. The increased volume of surgical procedures being done on an outpatient basis accounts for much of the growth in outpatient visits. The shift toward ambulatory surgery is not the only factor behind growth in hospital outpatient visits. Community hospitals have expanded the number and variety of outpatient services they provide.

INPATIENT COMPONENT

The third institutional component and the largest in terms of cost and personnel is the inpatient component. The inpatient element is measured by the number of hospital inpatients beds. Americans have asked the country's hospitals to provide a spectrum of inpatient care ranging from very sophisticated intensive care to minimal care, all of these types of care taking place within the hospital walls, using hospital beds. The inpatient component is the most costly in the system. Over the past decade, inpatient activity at community hospitals has fallen while the use of hospital outpatient services has increased dramatically. Many treatments and procedures that would have required an inpatient stay ten years ago are now routinely delivered in outpatient settings. As a result, fewer patients are being admitted to hospitals. Hospitals vary by ownership, purpose, and specialty. The most common hospital is the short-term community hospital. There are over 5,200 community hospitals. Hospitals operated by governments, whether state, federal, city, county, or district, are called governmental or municipal hospitals. There is a third category, referred to as specialty including long term care hospitals.

EXTENDED COMPONENT

This is the fourth element in the medical care system. Included in the extended component, but not limited to, are such services and institutions as home health care and hospice programs, end-stage renal disease programs, skilled nursing facilities called SNFs, and intermediate care facilities called ICFs. Together the SNFs and the ICFs are referred to as nursing homes. There are also assisted living facilities, personal care residences, rehabilitation hospitals, visiting nurses associations, and a more recent phenomenon called hospice care.

This extended component is expanding in breadth of services due mainly to the growth in the elderly and poor populations, both of which tend to suffer frequently from chronic conditions. This has resulted in a shift in focus from episodes of illness (such as admissions, visits, or length of stays) to continuous, comprehensive care management.

SPECIFIC ORGANIZATIONS AND WHERE ADMINISTRATORS WORK

Hospitals & Hospital Systems
- Corporate office specialists
- Functional/departments managers
- Senior hospital administrators
- System executives

Long-Term Care
- Adult day care
- Home care agencies
- Hospice programs
- Nursing homes

Care Related Areas
- Ambulatory care services
- Group medical practices
- Managed care organizations and insurance companies

Other Areas
- Association work
- College teaching
- Consulting
- State and local health departments
- University health services research

(Refer to Appendix D for samples of position openings.)

COMMUNITY AT LARGE COMPONENT

The fifth and final element in the medical care system is the noninstitutional component referred to as the community at large. The community is divided into three major groups. The first is comprised of the consumers-patients who use the health care facilities. The second group is comprised of the health personnel needed to staff the system. This includes a variety of training programs, and medical and nursing schools, as well as medicine's residency programs. Also included in this element are labor unions. Third, and perhaps the most powerful part of the community component, is the federal government, which pays for so much of the hospital care through the Medicare and Medicaid programs. The private insurance agency provides coverage for the majority of employed Americans. A key element under the community at large are the federal, state, local, and voluntary regulatory agencies. Much of the regulatory controls are focused on quality care and cost issues. Finally, the political system, the politics of health care that are behind so much of the legislation that governs the funding and direction of the health care system in this country.

In this outline of the five distinct components that make up our nation's medical care system one thing is very clear. The system tends to be a sickness care system more than a health care system. With the growth in managed care organizations this is starting to change. Each of the medical care components is part of a complex array of institutions and programs that involve people and countless other resources. And needless to say, these institutions and programs must be managed. It is the administrators of hospitals and managers of health care services that will perform these important managerial tasks.

CHAPTER 3

ADMINISTRATORS IN THE HOSPITAL

Health care is one of the largest industries in the country, and hospitals represent the largest fiscal component of this industry. But changes are impacting hospitals as never before. In 1993, 3.3 million people were admitted as inpatients to hospitals, the lowest number in twenty years. In the same year hospitals logged a total of 435 million outpatient visits, including physician office visits, same-day surgeries and home care visits. This continued a decade long trend in which ambulatory care rates soared by nearly 70 percent.

Hospital mergers and consolidations continue in virtually every geographic area of the country. In the past actual hospital closures were rare—but this also may change in the next five years. For the immediate future the forecast is for continually dwindling in-patient activities and burgeoning outpatient visits many of which will be provided in ambulatory centers off site from the parent hospital.

TYPES OF HOSPITALS

All hospitals are not alike. They may have different purposes and different functions. Essentially, hospitals take care of a patient's medical, surgical, psychiatric, and other illnesses and

Health Care Industry

	1994	%
EXPENDITURES (IN BILLIONS $)		
Hospital Care	$341.7	36.4%
Physician Services	182.7	19.5%
Dentist Services	40.0	4.3%
Nursing Home Care	74.2	7.9%
Drugs/Medical Supplies/Home Health Care	116.4	12.4%
Other Personal Health Care	77.6	8.3%
Other	105.7	11.3%
	$938.3	100.0%

Source: HCFA Office of the Actuary; Health Care Financing Review, Fall 1995.

injuries. The activities that are carried on in hospitals differ by the type of hospital. The kinds of medical and health personnel that work in hospitals differ by type of hospital as well. The basic difference between hospitals can be seen by how hospitals are classified. Fundamentally, a hospital can either be a community hospital or a noncommunity hospital. Our hospital industry is a mixture of both private and public hospitals. Hospitals have different types of ownership structure also. They may be organized for different purposes. Some are organized as voluntary (nonprofit) hospitals; others are organized to make a profit. Hospitals can be governed by community representatives or owned by a religious order. Hospitals can be classified as general medical-surgical hospitals or as specialty hospitals. Hospitals can be differentiated by how long the patient remains in the facility. Some hospitals are noted for medical education and teaching, and others have no teaching or research facilities. Hospitals are classified by the American Hospital Association as one of four types. A brief definition of the different types of hospitals follows:

1. General hospitals—The primary function of the institution is to provide patient services, diagnostic and therapeutic, for a variety of medical conditions.
2. Specialty hospitals—The primary function of the institution is to provide diagnostic and treatment services for patients who have specified medical conditions, both surgical and nonsurgical.
3. Rehabilitation and chronic disease hospitals—The primary function of the institution is provide diagnostic and treatment services to handicapped or disabled individuals requiring restorative and adjustive services.
4. Psychiatric hospitals—The primary function of the institution is to provide diagnostic and treatment services for patients who have psychiatric-related illnesses.

Hospitals are also classified by who owns or controls the institution. The different control classifications are as follows:

OWNERSHIP OF HOSPITALS

1. *GOVERNMENT, NONFEDERAL*
   - State
   - County
   - City
   - City-County
   - Hospital district or authority

2. *NONGOVERNMENT NOT-FOR-PROFIT*
   - Church operated
   - Other

3. *INVESTOR-OWNED (FOR-PROFIT)*
   - Individual
   - Partnership
   - Corporation

4. *GOVERNMENT, FEDERAL*
   • Air Force
   • Army
   • Navy
   • Public Health Service
   • Veteran's Administration

The primary mission of a hospital is patient care. However, there are other missions carried out in the hospital. An important one is the training and education of doctors, nurses, and health professionals. Another is the conducting of clinical research. These functions are usually carried out in larger institutions. More recently hospitals have become the focal point for the entire community's health care, offering a vast array of outpatient services as well as the traditional inpatient care. With this increasing emphasis on outpatient treatment, hospitals have been assuming an increasing role in preventive medicine. Hospitals have become the place in many communities where physicians, nurses, and other health care professionals pool their efforts to improve the public health of the community as well as treat illness. Public education, as a means of improving public health, is an important responsibility of the community hospital.

There are many kinds of hospitals. The most common, as we have noted, is the voluntary not-for-profit hospital, commonly referred to as a community hospital. There are two major categories of community hospitals: the teaching hospital, where nurses and doctors are trained, and the nonteaching community hospital. University hospitals and large medical centers are teaching institutions and emphasize education and research as well as service. These hospitals usually have very sophisticated clinical services. Both the federal government and state and local governments operate hospitals. Generally the federal government provides care for specific groups, such as the military, veterans, or even government employees. Many state and local hospitals are involved in psychiatric care and special health services for the poor.

Vital Statistics for Hospitals in the United States

SELECTED MEASURES IN COMMUNITY HOSPITALS,
1983 AND 1992–93

		Year		*Percent Change**	
MEASURE	1983	1992	1993	1983–93	1992–93
Hospitals	5,783	5,292	5,261	–9.0%	–0.6%
Beds (000s)	1,018	921	919	–9.8%	–0.2%
Average number of beds per hospital	176	174	175	–0.8%	0.4%
Admissions (000s)	36,152	31,034	30,748	–14.9%	–0.9%
Average daily census (000s)	749	604	592	–21.0%	–2.1%
Average length of stay, days	7.6	7.1	7.0	–7.1%	–1.4%
Inpatient days (000s)	273,197	221,047	215,889	–21.0%	–2.3%
Surgical operations (000s)	19,845	22,860	22,806	14.9%	–0.2%
Bassinets (000s)[a]	75	67	66	–12.5%	–1.5%
Births (000s)[a]	3,490	3,925	3,870	10.9%	–1.4%
Outpatient visits (000s)[b]	210,044	348,522	366,885	74.7%	5.3%

[a]Based only on hospitals reporting newborn data.

[b]Based only on hospitals reporting outpatient visits.

*Percent changes are based on actual figures, not rounded.

Source: *Hospital Statistics*, 1994 Edition, 1994 American Hospital Association Annual Survey Data, page xxxviii.

Finally there are investor-owned (for-profit) hospitals. These hospitals are owned by investors or private individuals for the purpose of gaining a return on their investment. These hospitals are usually community hospitals, though there are many proprietary psychiatric hospitals. Community hospitals are generally referred to as short-term, general, or acute hospitals. Generally, patients are admitted to these community, short-term hospitals for a stay not to exceed three weeks. Long-term hospitals, which often administer psychiatric care, may well keep patients an average of a month or even longer.

HIRING THE CHIEF EXECUTIVE OFFICER (CEO)

It is the board of trustees' responsibility to hire a competent, well-trained hospital administrator to lead the hospital. This may be the most important single task a board has to perform. Before hiring an administrator, the board undertakes a search (often seeking outside assistance) for the best person to lead their institution. Since hospitals are big business, trustees frequently seek administrators who have skills in business disciplines, including planning, organizing, and controlling. Communication and leadership skills are also strongly desirable. After hiring the administrator, the board delegates authority and responsibility for the institution's day-to-day operations to that individual. Though boards delegate sufficient authority for administrators to do their job, the trustees must retain the ultimate responsibility for all that occurs within the hospital. The formal relationship between a chief executive officer and the board of trustees is an employee-employer relationship. Successful administrators develop a partner relationship with their board. It is the board's responsibility to routinely guide, counsel, and evaluate its administrator, and if necessary, it is the board's responsibility to terminate the administrator.

Hospitals are very complex institutions. The governing body of most hospitals, as we have learned, is called the board of trustees, or the board of directors. The board has a chairperson, and it is the board's responsibility to head up the hospital, set policy, and select and hire the chief executive officer or administrator. The hospital is usually organized into major divisions, including the support, professional, fiscal, administrative, and nursing divisions. The hospital administrator, who may be called the president or executive director, is hired by the board of trustees and is held responsible for all aspects of the hospital's daily operations including the function of all its divisions.

Usually the administrator is called upon to rely on the physicians' and the medical staff's judgment in patient care matters and works closely with the chief of the medical staff. Most hospital administrators are specially trained for their position. Many university graduate programs are offered leading to a master's degree in health administration. There are also undergraduate programs that train hospital administrators.

SENIOR ADMINISTRATIVE STAFF

One of the most important responsibilities of the Chief Executive Officer (CEO) is to select and hire a competent administrative staff. It is the administrator's staff that is delegated the responsibility of seeing that the hospital is run smoothly and efficiently. Some of the key senior administrators include, Chief Financial Officer (CFO), Chief Nursing Officer (CNO), Chief Operating Officer (COO), and Chief Medical Officer (CMO). The hospital also includes department managers in the many nonmedical departments such as personnel, medical records, dietary control, housekeeping, and purchasing. The purchasing agent, frequently called the materials manager, is also a key department head whose duty it is to order supplies for maintaining logistical support within the hospital. The public relations director is an important arm of the management team and the board in reaching out to the community. The personnel director, now usually called the human

A Typical Hospital Organization Chart

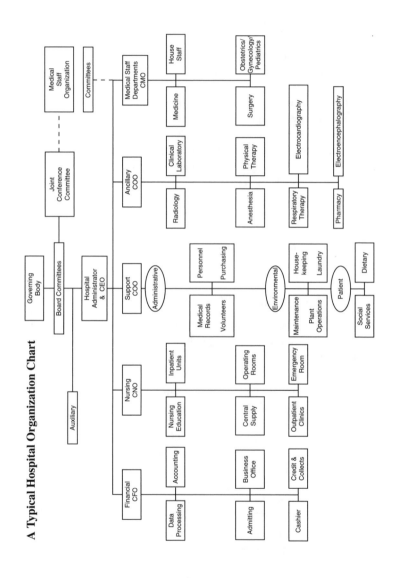

resources director, is critical in selecting and orienting hospital personnel as well as guiding the hospital administrator on personnel matters. The hospital business manager and controller are also key individuals in maintaining the hospital's financial records. The management information department and its manager have become an important ingredient in the modern hospital.

JOB SUMMARIES AND COMPENSATION

Chief Executive Officer (CEO)/Administrator

Job Summary: Responsible for overall functioning of organization and for adherence to organization's mission. Develops and implements strategic plans for maintaining and/or improving delivery of services.

Compensation:	Average salary	$169.2
(in thousands)	Average bonus	$50.0
	Average total compensation	$179.8
	Bonus eligible	21.2%
	Bonus as % of salary	20.9%

Chief Operations Officer (COO)/Administrative Officer

Job Summary: Responsible for day-to-day operations carried out by the organization. Acts in place of CEO/Administrator when CEO is not available.

Compensation:	Average salary	$123.7
(in thousands)	Average bonus	$29.1
	Average total compensation	$130.7
	Bonus eligible	23.9%
	Bonus as % of salary	16.5%

Chief Financial Officer (CFO)

Job Summary: Responsible for developing and implementing organization's financial plan and for implementing accounting and budgeting policies. Directs processes whereby departments develop budgets, track expenses, record and collect revenue, and maintain financial statements.

Compensation:	Average salary	$106.3
(in thousands)	Average bonus	$19.4
	Average total compensation	$110.7
	Bonus eligible	22.8%
	Bonus as % of salary	13.9%

Chief Medical Officer (CMO)/Medical Director

Job Summary: Directs medical staff planning, recruitment, and development. Acts as liaison between administration and medical staffs. Implements organization's policies with respect to delivery of medical services.

Compensation:	Average salary	$143.6
(in thousands)	Average bonus	$21.9
	Average total compensation	$146.4
	Bonus eligible	12.7%
	Bonus as % of salary	14.0%

Chief Nursing Officer (CNO)

Job Summary: Directs nursing staff planning, recruitment, and development. Coordinates activities of nursing staff with those of other areas. Implements organization's policies with respect to delivery of nursing services. Oversees nursing budget.

Compensation:	Average salary	$82.0
(in thousands)	Average bonus	$12.2
	Average total compensation	$84.5
	Bonus eligible	20.3%
	Bonus as % of salary	11.8%

Source: Copyright 1996 by Coopers & Lybrand L.L.P., Published by the Survey/Research Unit, Human Resource Advisory, Coopers & Lybrand.

CHAPTER 4

DEPARTMENTAL ADMINISTRATORS IN THE HOSPITAL

The opportunities for administration in a hospital are not limited to the few executive jobs at the top; many other challenging and diversified management jobs exist in today's hospital. Because of rapid continuing growth in the health care field and the trend toward specialization, many new administrative positions must be filled to effectively operate today's hospital. Scientific and medical gains have had an impact on all health professions and occupations, including those in management. Some management positions require a degree of technical knowledge, but many can be learned with a combination of formal schooling and on-the-job experience. One example is the executive housekeeper. Other administrative jobs offer specialists practical experience in their primary occupations as well as the opportunity to manage people and other resources. Nurses, pharmacists, accountants, and many other professionals are all candidates for this type of administrative position.

Certain key hospital departmental administrative positions will be reviewed by following the general functions of a hospital as outlined in the typical hospital organization chart outlined in

Chapter 3. The managerial positions will be divided into four general categories. The first is finance; second, support and administrative services; third, management in nursing service; and fourth, planning and marketing.

SELECTED HOSPITAL DEPARTMENTAL ADMINISTRATORS

FINANCIAL AREA

- The Hospital Controller
- The Business Office Manager
- Hospital Credit Manager
- Director of Admissions
- Director of Information Systems
- Manager of Managed Care

SUPPORT AREA

- Director of Human Resources
- Purchasing Director/Materials Manager
- Director of Food Service
- Executive Housekeeper
- Director of Medical Records
- Director of Volunteer Services

NURSING AREA

- Unit Managers
- Risk Manager
- Quality Assurance Director

PLANNING AND MARKETING AREA

- Director of Marketing
- Director of Public Relations
- Director of Planning
- Director of Development

ADMINISTRATORS IN FINANCE

The majority of the financial management specialist's duties focus on financial analysis. The financial management specialist is also responsible for accounting and capital, and department budgeting and auditing.

Managing finances in a hospital involves much more than simply keeping track of what funds come into and go out of the institution. The hospital administrator has to know at all times how the hospital is operating as a business. Quality of care must be maintained at high standards. Appropriate fees must be charged for services of all degrees of complexity. Knowing the appropriate amount to charge for service is an administrator's job, and the financial managers carry out the responsibility of these decisions. Financial management is part of the detailed system that establishes appropriate fees for services and determines how they should be recorded and reported.

With the rapid growth of third party (insurance) payers such as Blue Cross, and managed care organizations and particularly with the increase in the Medicare program, financial management has taken on new importance. Because many hospitals do not operate to generate a profit as most retail businesses do, there are many unique, interesting aspects of hospital financial management. Many traditional business systems that are used in a purely profit-making business may not be appropriate in the nonprofit hospital. This added dimension means that the men and women who select hospital financial management as a career must be bright and motivated and have the ability to be innovative.

The administrators who manage the monies in the hospital keep the institution alive. With proper management of funds, the hospital is able to pay nurses and doctors, provide services to the community, purchase needed medical supplies and equipment, and continue to add to its buildings and facilities.

There are administrative careers at all levels of hospital financial management. They include the following.

The Hospital Controller

Description of work: The controller is the head of the fiscal division of the hospital. The controller is responsible for the entire area of the institution's financial management including budgeting, bookkeeping, general accounting activities, crediting, and collecting on patients' bills. The controller generally reports directly to the hospital administrator. Reporting to the controller are several financial department heads including the business office manager, the accountant, and the hospital's patient accounts manager. Having delegated certain key responsibilities, the controller spends time establishing appropriate financial reporting and accounting systems. The controller may work closely with both the hospital administrator and the board of trustees, informing these parties of the institution's financial status and its future trends in this area.

In order to accomplish job duties, the controller works closely with the various hospital departmental managers. As part of his or her job, the controller recommends different ways to improve the fiscal operation of their departments, including recommendations to increase revenues and decrease costs.

Educational requirements and skills: A bachelor's degree in accounting or business administration is the minimum educational requirement. Experience after college in progressively responsible accounting or finance positions, preferably within a hospital, is also needed. Some supervisory responsibility would be helpful, as would coursework in hospital administration. Certain hospitals might require state certification as a certified public accountant (CPA). Often controllers have been promoted from the position of senior accountant or business office manager.

Compensation:	Average salary	$67.4
	Average bonus	$9.7
	Average total compensation	$68.9
	Bonus eligible	15.8%
	Bonus as % of salary	11.2%

Director, Patient Accounts

Description of work: This person supervises the patients' accounts branch of the hospital's financial area. The position may also be titled manager of patient accounts. The credit manager is responsible for coordinating and supervising the hospital credit and collection department. The credit manager or members of the staff direct the institution's collection effort by interviewing hospital patients, both inpatients and outpatients, and determining their ability to pay for the services they received or may receive. Facts and information are gathered during a credit interview which relate to the patient's pay scale, present job, past credit record, and any debts or loans the patient may have. The credit manager may also run various credit references on the patient. It is the manager's responsibility to explain the hospital's credit and collection policy to the patient or next of kin, and then if necessary, to aid the patient in working out a payment plan.

Educational requirements and skills: A college degree or some college courses in either business administration or accounting are considered desirable. Several years' experience in credit and collection work is preferred by most hospitals.

Compensation:	Average salary	$52.4
	Average bonus	$4.0
	Average total compensation	$52.8
	Bonus eligible	10.3%
	Bonus as % of salary	6.7%

Director of Admissions

Description of work: The admitting officer may be the first employee the patient has contact with when coming to the hospital. The admitting officer is in charge of the admitting department and is responsible for supervising and coordinating all the departmental operations. The department head usually works with assistants called admitting clerks. One of the manager's main functions is to select, train, and supervise the admitting personnel. The department is held accountable for all the various steps a patient must go through prior to being admitted to the hospital. The admitting staff assigns the patient a room, notifies other hospital departments of the admission, and takes all the administrative and clerical data for the patient's medical record. The admitting staff also explains the hospital's rules and procedures to the patient. They may also obtain signatures on certain release or permission forms. The department must keep current information on patient room assignments and transfers.

Educational requirements and skills: A college degree in business administration or a social science would be helpful. One or two years of prior work in an admitting department is required. Some hospitals may employ a nurse as the admitting officer.

Compensation:

Average salary	$44.5
Average bonus	$4.4
Average total compensation	$45.0
Bonus eligible	10.8%
Bonus as % of salary	8.1%

Data Processing Manager

Description of work: The manager of the hospital's data processing department is responsible for coordinating all functions of this information processing department. The department uses computers and other electronic data processing applications. The operations of the data processing department are constantly changing because of improvements in computers (hardware) and computer programs (software). The functions of this department are quite complex. One of the major functions of the data processing manager is to advise management on new information systems and to inform the other hospital department heads about the various financial and statistical reports generated from the data processing area. The data processing manager is responsible for all three main functions in the department: the planning, programming, and processing of data and information.

Educational requirements and skills: Computer science is a highly technical and specialized area; therefore, this position usually requires a bachelor's degree in computer science, accounting, or mathematics. Some experience in programming and systems work is also helpful. Several years' experience in computer-related work will generally be required before assuming the manager's position.

Compensation:	Average salary	$72.9
	Average bonus	$12.1
	Average total compensation	$74.6
	Bonus eligible	14.2%
	Bonus as % of salary	11.8%

Director of Managed Care

Description of work: The director directs and coordinates the development of managed care strategies and activities for a medical center and its affiliates. This person advises and consults with operating departments to handle managed care requirements in terms of UR, billing, registration, etc. The director also coordinates with practice groups and clinical departments managed care opportunities for specific services and programs such as EAP, occupational health, and substance abuse services.

Compensation:	Average salary	$74.4
	Average bonus	$3.5
	Average total compensation	$75.0
	Bonus eligible	16.3%
	Bonus as % of salary	5.7%

ADMINISTRATORS IN SUPPORT SERVICES

The support services in a hospital represent the functions that support the medical and nursing divisions in the institution. The support services include three general functional areas: environmental services, including the housekeeping and maintenance departments; administrative services, including the personnel and purchasing departments; and patient-service areas, including the pharmacy and social service departments. All the support departments require detailed management if they are to operate efficiently and contribute to the hospital's mission of patient care. The following is a selected list of administrative positions available in the hospital support services.

Director of Human Resources

Description of work: This person manages the hospital's personnel department functions. This department head is responsible for the recruitment, selection, and placement of employees within the institution. The personnel director has the responsibilities of developing personnel policies and procedures on working conditions, employment practices, pay scales, and grievance procedures. The personnel department is also responsible for providing employee orientation programs and establishing training programs.

Educational requirements and skills: A bachelor's degree is generally required with a major in business administration, personnel administration, or industrial relations. Work toward a master's degree will enable a person to advance more rapidly. Courses in tests and measurements as well as applied psychology are helpful. The ability to analyze job situations and to effectively communicate with people is important in this position.

Compensation:	Average salary	$71.6
	Average bonus	$10.7
	Average total compensation	$73.6
	Bonus eligible	18.3%
	Bonus as % of salary	10.5%

Purchasing Director/Materials Manager

Description of work: Purchasing is a basic function in any business. However, in the hospital business it takes on greater dimension and importance. Hospitals need a wide variety of supplies, materials, and equipment because of the range of clinical situations handled in the institution. In the hospital field there is also constant change and growth in the number, kind, and sophistication of medical supplies and equipment. The pace of change in this area is perhaps faster than in any other industry. This means the job of a hospital purchasing director is stimulating and exciting. The purchasing director is responsible for supervising and directing a program to purchase the necessary supplies, materials, and equipment to keep the hospital functioning properly. This involves supervising the storage, control, and issuance of supplies to the various hospital departments. The director must also maintain contacts with the hospital's vendors and keep up to date on prices, trends, and the availability of supplies and new products.

Educational requirements and skills: Usually the position calls for a manager who has graduated from college with a degree in business administration or a related field. Courses in accounting, marketing, and purchasing are helpful. Knowledge of applied business economics and business practices is also desirable.

Compensation:	Average salary	$52.8
	Average bonus	$5.6
	Average total compensation	$53.4
	Bonus eligible	11.0%
	Bonus as % of salary	8.4%

Food Service Administrator

In some ways, hospitals are very much like large restaurants. They must prepare and serve meals to patients and staff. But unlike restaurants, the food prepared in the hospital may well play a role in a patient's recovery. Many developments have occurred in dietary research over the last fifty years. Science has given us new tools and methods to measure people's food needs. It has shown us the role various nutrients play in making us healthy.

Description of work: The food service administrator may also be called the administrative dietician. It is this department head's job to direct and coordinate the food preparation for the hospital. The manager is also responsible for the preparation of special diets for patients. Responsibilities also include supervising personnel, requisitioning food and supplies, and maintaining records.

Educational requirements and skills: The food service administrator should have a college degree in nutrition, business administration, or a related field. Being familiar with large-scale food operations like those found in universities and hospitals is also necessary. An understanding of quality controls in the purchasing and preparation of food is desirable.

Compensation:	Average salary	$49.2
	Average bonus	$3.3
	Average total compensation	$49.5
	Bonus eligible	10.3%
	Bonus as % of salary	5.7%

Executive Housekeeper

Description of work: There are very few things more important in the day-to-day administration of a hospital than keeping it clean. The supervision and direction of the institution's housekeeping program is the responsibility of the executive housekeeper. The person in this management position must set the standards of cleanliness throughout the hospital. Establishing work methods and systems, preparing cleaning schedules, and hiring and training the housekeeping department employees are part of this administrator's job. The hospital's laundry service may also be part of this person's responsibility.

Educational requirements and skills: To be certified for membership in the National Executive Housekeepers' Association, it is necessary to hold a high school diploma. College courses in management are also helpful. Knowledge of the hospital's operations and a thorough understanding of building materials and equipment are important in this position. Supervision of employees is a key part of this manager's role.

Compensation: Average salary $43.2
             Average bonus $3.1
             Average total compensation $46.3
             Bonus eligible   10.6%
             Bonus as % of salary   6.3%

Director of Volunteer Services

There has been a significant role expansion for hospital volunteers over the last several years. Volunteers are no longer restricted to working in the hospital snack bar or to manning the hospitality cart. Today's volunteers can be found in all areas of the hospital—covering the telephone switchboard, serving as patient-care representatives, acting as substitute mothers on the pediatric unit, and generally supporting the hospital in its mission. Volunteers are also found working on outreach projects and serving under the auspices of a hospital auxiliary to aid the hospital in fund-raising activities. There is a whole new era of hospital voluntarism today, and the volunteer department needs administration.

Description of work: The director of volunteer services, or the director of volunteers, directs and coordinates the effort of the volunteers in the hospital. To do this, the department head must establish a volunteer program in conjunction with the various hospital departments that use volunteer services. The director of the volunteer department organizes formal instructional programs for volunteers in order to orient and teach them proper hospital procedures and techniques. At times, this departmental administrator will suggest and supervise projects to be completed by the volunteers.

Educational requirements and skills: Usually the director of this department has a college education. It could be helpful to have taken courses in management, sociology, and psychology. Training in public relations and public speaking would be very helpful in this position. Most hospitals prefer that their director of volunteers have some supervisory experience, experience as a volunteer, and/or have participated in some community organization work.

Compensation:	Average salary	$38.4
	Average bonus	$2.9
	Average total compensation	$38.6
	Bonus eligible	8.9%
	Bonus as % of salary	6.8%

ADMINISTRATORS IN NURSING

Nursing in the modern hospital is carried out in separate areas called nursing units. The organization of the nursing unit is an achievement of many years' development. The person in charge of the nursing unit is called the head nurse. The responsibilities carried out by the head nurse are broad and complex, for a nursing unit is a microcosm of the entire hospital. The head nurse must carry out policies and procedures, cope with crises with patients and staff, attend to routine floor administration, and relate to the patients' visitors.

To help the head nurses in their management of the nursing units, some hospitals employ unit managers or floor managers.

Top Nursing Officer

Description of work: The top nursing officer directs nursing staff planning recruitment and development. This person coordinates activities of nursing staff with those of other areas, implements organization's policies with respect to delivery of nursing services, and oversees the nursing budget.

Compensation:	Average salary	$82.0
	Average bonus	$12.2
	Average total compensation	$84.5
	Bonus eligible	20.3%
	Bonus as % of salary	11.8%

Care or Case Manager

Description of work: The case manager identifies inpatients at high risk of re-admission and works with patients during inpatient stay to achieve maximum independence upon discharge. The manager develops the multidisciplinary care plan (critical paths) in collaboration with other members of the health care team, and coordinates with social workers to arrange community support services for high risk patients following discharge. He or she also provides support and counseling to patient and family.

Compensation: Average salary $42.1
                  Average bonus   —
                  Average total compensation $42.1
                  Bonus eligible   0.0%
                  Bonus as % of salary   —

Risk Manager

The hospital has a great deal of liability for clinical practice. This has been established by the courts and laws of various states. The hospital has a duty to keep its patients free from harm. To reduce the hospital's liability and also to provide a safe environment for its patients and staff, hospitals use a logical and systematic approach called a risk management program. Risk management is a relatively new discipline.

Description of work: The hospital risk manager is a member of the administration who works closely with the nursing service and the nursing units. It is the manager's job to implement and coordinate the institution's risk management program. The manager uses insurance company reports, hospital incident reports, licensing and accrediting agencies' surveys and audits, as well as his or her own inspections in order to structure ways the hospital can lower its risk and improve its environment. Orientation and training sessions for staff are part of this person's role.

Compensation: Average salary $55.4
                  Average bonus $4.0
                  Average total compensation $55.7
                  Bonus eligible   9.0%
                  Bonus as % of salary   7.0%

Quality Assurance Director

The concept of quality assurance has been well established in manufacturing industries for many years, but only recently has it been adopted by hospitals. Considerable attention has been placed on quality in medical care by consumers and review agencies. The courts have also placed hospitals on notice that they must assure the quality of care in their institutions. As a result of the Medicare law, hospitals started utilization review programs in 1966, and later, in the 1970s, began medical audit programs. These are two major components of a hospital's quality assurance effort.

Description of work: The quality assurance director, who may also be called a utilization coordinator, is in charge of the hospital's quality assurance program. This department head will maintain a system of control over the utilization of the facility, including monitoring the patient's length of stay and the appropriateness of services the patient has received. The department will publish criteria for medical audit and reviews. The director will work with the various hospital and medical staff committees to review and improve patient care. The manager will retain records and profiles on patient care and utilization studies performed.

Educational requirements and skills: A master's degree in hospital administration or a related field is usually considered a minimum requirement. A degree in a related field such as nursing is also acceptable. A broad knowledge of medical terminology is required. Good judgment and the ability to deal with people at all levels in the institution is very helpful.

Compensation:

Average salary	$55.3
Average bonus	$4.0
Average total compensation	$55.7
Bonus eligible	9.2%
Bonus as % of salary	7.0%

ADMINISTRATORS IN PLANNING AND MARKETING

Director of Marketing

Description of work: The marketing and program planning specialist is responsible for projects and tasks relating to market research, planning, and promotion; interpretation of patient/customer/physician attitudes, values, and expectations; assessment of current programs, and testing of the clinical, operational, financial, ethical, medical, and legal feasibility of proposed programs. Services which may be provided include those involving high-tech equipment, medical programs such as organ transplantation, burn centers, airborne medical evacuation services, and hospice programs.

Compensation:	Average salary	$75.4
	Average bonus	$11.8
	Average total compensation	$77.4
	Bonus eligible	16.5%
	Bonus as % of salary	13.1%

Director of Planning

Description of work: The director of planning develops marketing plans for organization, including plans for new services and adaption of existing services to better serve the client population.

Compensation:	Average salary	$80.0
	Average bonus	$15.6
	Average total compensation	$84.2
	Bonus eligible	26.8%
	Bonus as % of salary	13.3%

PUBLIC RELATIONS

Director Public Relations

Description of work: The director implements organization's community and public relations activities, including advertising, marketing, and press releases.

Compensation:		
	Average salary	$49.8
	Average bonus	$4.5
	Average total compensation	$50.1
	Bonus eligible	7.5%
	Bonus as % of salary	8.2%

Director of Development

Description of work: It is the communication and fund-raising specialist's job to develop programs which will increase the amount of political, community, and financial support. Other duties include planning and implementing fund-raising efforts, such as specific projects and activities that are a part of annual or capital campaigns, as well as evaluating fund-raising programs. This position requires excellent communication tools and techniques and the ability to assess constituency, consumer attitudes, expectations, and level of support.

Compensation:		
	Average salary	$64.3
	Average bonus	$10.5
	Average total compensation	$65.7
	Bonus eligible	13.2%
	Bonus as % of salary	13.4%

CHAPTER 5

ADMINISTRATORS IN RELATED AREAS

Now that we have reviewed the administrators in the hospital setting and where senior administrators and other managers fit into the hospital organization, we will look at certain other health care organizations and work settings that are available for health care related administrators.

HEALTH CARE RELATED ORGANIZATIONS

1. Multihospital and Integrated Delivery Systems
2. Group Practice Management
3. Management Service Organizations (MSOs)
4. Managed Care Organizations (MCOs)/Health Maintenance Organizations (HMOs)
5. Ambulatory Services
6. Behavioral Medicine and Mental Health
7. Long-Term Care Institutions
8. Insurance Companies
9. Consultants
10. Other Health Care Agencies

MULTIHOSPITAL AND INTEGRATED
DELIVERY SYSTEMS

Entities made up of two or more hospitals, more commonly known as multihospital systems, supply many opportunities to today's managers. These systems no longer operate only hospitals, but also nursing homes, psychiatric hospitals, health maintenance organizations, preferred provider organizations, and other free-standing facilities. When a hospital system broadens its range of services to include such services, they then are referred to as Integrated Delivery Systems. The management team of multihospital systems plays important roles in financing and marketing their subsidiaries' services, and acquiring goods and services for them as well. Multihospital systems continue to increase. According to surveys multihospitals systems to be a dominant market force by year 2000.

GROUP PRACTICE MANAGEMENT

A medical group practice is a formal association of three or more physicians and possibly certain other health care professionals, such as optometrists, podiatrists, nurse practitioners, or physical therapists, who provide patient services. The income generated initially from this medical practice is pooled and then redistributed to the members in the group practice under some prearranged plan. Often these associations are partnerships or a legal entity called a professional corporation. The group practice concept is beneficial to doctors, since by grouping together they save on various overhead expenses in running a practice. Group practices can be organized in different ways.

The larger groups require business managers or administrators to aid them in their practice. A group practice may even own its private clinic facility. Business managers of group practices may belong to the Medical Group Management Association (MGMA), formerly known as the National Association of Clinic Managers. Much like the hospital administrator, the medical group practice manager must be familiar with finances, and in particular, patient accounts. Handling records and procedures as well as understanding personnel administration is important in this job. Also, the professional medical group manager is inevitably involved in a great many matters related to the medical staff. The concept of group practice should continue to grow since it is quite difficult for a solo practitioner to keep up with the current technology, health care regulations, and ever-changing methods of reimbursement. And as in so many growth industries, there will be a demand for qualified administrators.

MANAGEMENT SERVICE ORGANIZATIONS (MSOs)

Health care organizations everywhere are recognizing the competitive necessity and high value of leveraging administrative services to physicians through Management Services Organizations (MSOs). In addition to professional management of routine medical office functions such as billing and accounts receivable, the MSO can be of enormous help in tackling the many challenges of managed care. In order for the MSO to be successful, it must negotiate often thorny politics, earn the acceptance and support of a diverse medical community, build an excellent infrastructure and be cost-efficient. Offered services vary dramatically from one MSO to the next, but virtually all MSOs include some electronic infrastructure.

MANAGED CARE ORGANIZATIONS (MCOs) AND HEALTH MAINTENANCE ORGANIZATIONS (HMOs)

A Managed Care Organization (MCO) refers to any type of organizational entity providing managed care such as an HMO. The first public appearance of the term *health maintenance organization* (HMO) was on March 23, 1970, when the Department of Health, Education and Welfare presented the administration with a health cost effectiveness bill that went before the House Ways and Means Committee. There was no specific organization outline at the time, but rather, a general concept of a health maintenance contract. Later, in 1973, in a report from the committee on interstate and foreign commerce of the HMO Act, Public Law 93–222 was launched. At that time an HMO was legally defined. An HMO is responsible for providing most health and medical care services required by enrolled individuals or families. These services are specified in the contract between the persons or family enrolled and the organization company, the HMO.

At present there are over 500 HMOs with 50 million members or enrollees. This is an increase of 69 percent over the last two years. The federal government projects a continued rapid rise in HMO enrollment in the next several years. From these statistics you can see that this is an excellent area for future growth opportunities for health administrators.

AMBULATORY SERVICES

The challenge of Ambulatory Services management also involves managing the needs of patients and many physicians and other providers working in the same physical facility. Many of these providers use the same resources, supplies, and laboratory, and also share nursing and clinic nonprofessional staff. As is evident, this type of setting requires confident management and tact in dealing with people. Ambulatory managers often work in decentralized sites (freestanding) away from the parent organizations.

BEHAVIORAL MEDICINE AND MENTAL HEALTH

In 1956, Congress, with the urging of President Dwight D. Eisenhower, established the Joint Commission on Mental Illness in Health. It was this commission's final report that gave impetus to the growth of community mental health services in this country. The report recommended an end to the construction of very large mental health (psychiatric) hospitals and suggested that a flexible array of services be provided in the community for mental illness. In 1963, Congress showed continued concern when it passed the Mental Retardation Facilities and Community Mental Health Centers Construction Act of 1963 (Public Law 88–164). It was this act, and subsequent amendments to the act, that provided federal assistance to public and nonprofit facilities for the construction and staffing of community mental health centers in this country. Today there are hundreds of such comprehensive mental centers in the United States.

The management of behavioral medicine activities is similar to the management of a hospital's ambulatory services. A mental health administrator has to deal with many different types of professionals, including psychiatrists, psychologists, and social workers. There is heavy professional staffing in mental health centers. Today's world of community mental health centers seems to indicate that centers are moving toward an ever-increasing scope of professional resources with even larger and more diverse staffs. With such diverse staffs comes an increasingly complex organizational structure. This is a special challenge for the mental health administrator. A mental health administrator must be ready for close involvement with the government at all levels, as well as with the community in which the facility is located.

LONG-TERM CARE INSTITUTIONS

Long-term care refers to physical and mental health services provided to temporarily or chronically disabled persons over an extended period of time with a goal of enabling them to maintain as high as possible a level of independent functioning. The basic difference between long-term care management and the administration of general hospitals rests in the nature of the patients' problems. In the long-term setting the institution's medical, nursing, and support services are all geared to patients whose physical and/or mental problems call for institutionalization over many months or even years.

Many management opportunities exist in the country's nursing homes. Today many health administration programs offer long-term care concentrations at the master's degree level. *Nursing homes* are generally defined as the wide range of institutions which offer a variety of levels of care. Nursing home includes freestanding institutions which offer nursing service and related services from the skilled nursing facility down to residential care.

Opportunities for management also can be found in related long-term institutional care, such as adult daycare, hospice programs, and home health care services. Home health agencies provide health care and supportive services to the disabled in their homes. They are enjoying a rapid growth in popularity. The range of services offered by home health care is similar to that in the nursing home. For example, physical therapy, personal care, and homemaker's services are all available.

INSURANCE COMPANIES

The insurance industry is also a valuable resource for those seeking a position in health care management The insurance industry works very closely with hospitals, nursing homes, and other institutions, as well as with doctors. The first health insurance plan in America started in 1929, when a group of school teachers in cooperation with Baylor Hospital in Dallas, Texas, made monthly payments in exchange for hospital coverage. From this seed grew the Blue Cross plans. There are presently seventy Blue Cross plans in the country. All of these plans provide specific services related to the writing and administration of health care benefits across the country. Consequently, the Blue Cross plans also offer numerous opportunities for the prospective health care administrator. It is also interesting to note that in many parts of the country, Blue Cross plans act as intermediaries for the Medicare program.

Career opportunities also exist in the physician's counterpart to Blue Cross, the Blue Shield plans. Blue Shield is associated with Blue Cross even though it is a separate organization. Blue Shield plans cover more than sixty-five million Americans and are also involved in the Medicare-Medicaid programs as carriers under the doctor portion of that legislation. The graduate of a health administration program who goes into the public insurance field will quickly see how valuable public relations skills are in negotiating claims between companies and hospitals. The graduate will also value training in actuarial and rate-setting procedures.

CONSULTANTS

The complex world of management and its other related administrative challenges, planning, association work, and insurance, all require from time to time outside assistance of some nature. It is the health administrator as a consultant who meets this need. The consultant can bring a fresh approach or perspective to solving administrative problems. Consultants identify problems and recommend ways of solving them.

Consultants have been increasingly used in the health field and particularly by the government at all levels. Not only can a consultant bring a new perspective to a situation, but his or her problem-solving proposals are frequently the most cost-effective means of getting a difficult task accomplished. Since consultants are often requested to solve very technical problems, a graduate going into this field will need certain skills, such as a working knowledge of accounting, information systems, organization, and communications.

OTHER HEALTH CARE AGENCIES

The federal government is the largest employer of health personnel in the country. Accordingly, there are many opportunities for health administration careers at a variety of governmental levels. Within the federal government, the Public Health Service and many other major governmental agencies such as the National Institutes of Health (NIH); Center for Disease Control (CDC); Human Resource Administration (HRA); Health Services Administration (HSA); Food and Drug Administration (FDA); and the Alcohol, Drug Abuse, and Mental Health Administration (ADAMHA), have extensive programs that require trained health management professionals to administrate them. These agencies are in addition to the branches of the armed forces and veterans administration, which maintain health programs as well as their own system of hospitals. The government offers a major segment of management employment to health care administrators.

There are many opportunities in health planning for trained health administrators. For many recent graduates from health administration programs, health planning has provided an attractive alternative to institutional management levels, especially where hospitals in the same region have formed hospital councils.

CHAPTER 6

THE CARE OF THE ELDERLY

FACTS ON AGING

There is a major change underway in our country. America has a population which is rapidly growing older. Never before has this country had so many older citizens.

These older groups have many problems. Income, or lack of, is one of them. Retirement at sixty-five usually brings a reduction in income, yet the need for medical services tends to increase with advancing age. Inflationary pressures put a squeeze on older citizens. Living arrangements also become a problem for the elderly. As people become older, especially beyond age sixty-five, the number of individuals living in a family unit decreases rapidly. Another problem for the aged is their need for comprehensive health care and medical services. The acute medical care given by hospitals and skilled nursing homes is taken care of, for the most part, by the Medicare program, but other portions of care—particularly for the chronically and terminally ill—are not paid for adequately. The majority of the "Most Frail Elderly" are over 85.

Distribution of the Elderly Population by Age, 1990–2025

	1990		2000 Projections		2025 Projections	
Age	*No.*	*%*	*No.*	*%*	*No.*	*%*
All 65 years and over	31,799	100.0	35,036	100.0	58,636	100.0
65–69	10,006	31.5	9,110	26.0	18,314	31.2
70–74	8,048	25.3	8,583	24.5	14,774	25.2
75–79	6,224	19.6	7,242	20.7	11,103	18.9
80–84	4,060	12.8	4,565	14.2	6,767	11.5
85+	3,461	10.9	5,136	14.7	7,678	13.1

There is a wide range of services and institutions meeting the medical health and needs of the elderly. It is a dynamic sector of the medical care system that demands innovative planning and administration. Challenging administrative positions are available in this area.

SERVICES AND INSTITUTIONS
Adult Day Health Center

Definition: Adult Day Health Center sometimes referred to as Adult Day Care serves both clients and their caregivers. Clients receive nursing/medical care and/or therapies and participate in stimulating social and recreational activities with peers. Caregivers receive the respite they need, along with education and counseling.

Alzheimer's (Dementia) Care Unit

Definition: The objectives of dementia care are as follows:
1. To provide secure shelter, warmth and food.
2. To support those abilities not totally impaired by dementia.

3. To ensure an appropriate range of environmental and sensual stimulation and information.
4. To support and reinforce each resident's understanding of his or her place in time or space.
5. To create unobtrusive opportunities for social interaction.
6. To maintain an individual's right to privacy.
7. To emphasize links with the past and the familiar with a homelike setting.
8. To provide opportunities that support programs for wandering.
9. To define spaces into public, shared, semi-private, private, and staff.
10. To allow for future change and changing needs.

People over 85 who need help...

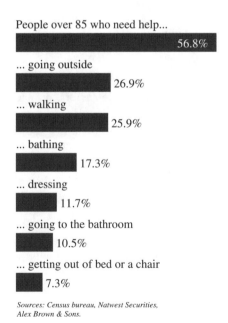

56.8%

... going outside

26.9%

... walking

25.9%

... bathing

17.3%

... dressing

11.7%

... going to the bathroom

10.5%

... getting out of bed or a chair

7.3%

Sources: Census bureau, Natwest Securities, Alex Brown & Sons.

Assisted Living Facilities

Definition: Senior living complex with physical features designed to assist the frail elderly, with staff personnel and programs that assist residents with the activities of daily living. Units may or may not have kitchens, however, meals are provided in a central location. Units also usually rent on a monthly basis.

Comprehensive Outpatient Rehabilitation Facility (CORF)

Definition: A CORF is a nonresidential facility that is established and operated exclusively for the purpose of providing diagnostic, therapeutic, and restorative services to outpatients for the rehabilitation of injured, disabled, or sick persons, at a single fixed location, by or under the supervision of a physician.

Congregate Care Facilities

Definition: A multifamily complex catering to seniors, primarily single women with a common dining facility. Units have small kitchens for casual use. Limited support services such as linen service, housekeeping, transportation, and social activities may or may not be provided. Units also usually rent on a monthly basis.

Continuing Care Retirement Communities (CCRC)

Definition: A senior living complex providing a continuum of care including housing, health care, and various support services. Health care (i.e., nursing) services may be provided for directly or through access to affiliated health care facilities. Fees structured either as a refundable entry fee, plus a monthly fee; as a condominium; as a rental; or as an endowment; may require mandatory insurance.

The CCRC is also known under the term "life care center." Initially Life Care Center became prevalent in the Northeast, while the term CCRC was used widely in the western regions of the country.

Home Health Care

Definition: A coordinated program that provides medical care, nursing and additional treatment and social services to patients in their place of residence.

Hospice/Hospice Care

Definition: A program providing palliative care—primarily medical relief of pain and symptoms management—and support services to terminally ill patients, as well as assistance to their families in adjusting to the patient's illness and death.

Hospital-Based Skilled Nursing Facility

Definition: Provides medical and continuous nursing care services to nonacute patients who mainly require convalescent, rehabilitative and/or restorative services. May be located on or off of the hospital campus, but must meet the following three criteria: 1) both the hospital and the nursing home must be governed by a common governing board; 2) hospital and nursing home must file a common Medicare cost report; and 3) the nursing home must obtain more than half of its services from the hospital.

Independent Living Facilities

Definition: A multifamily complex catering to active seniors, mostly couples, who are able to function independently. Support services, if offered are hospitality-related. Apartments may rent on a monthly basis or may have a condominium, cooperative for fee simple title structure.

Intermediate Care

Definition: Health-related services that are provided to individuals who do not require hospital or skilled nursing care, but whose condition requires services that are above the level of room and board and can be made available only in an inpatient setting.

Membership Packages for Seniors

Definition: Hospitals or other provider organizations that offer extra benefits to consumers who join such programs for older consumers. Seniors are offered a wide range of benefits, including assistance in filling out Medicare and insurance forms, discounts on drugs and on meals in the hospital cafeterias and referrals to physicians who will not change patients beyond what Medicare pays.

Nursing Homes

Definition: That grouping of extended care facilities referred to a "Nursing Home." Nursing homes is a broad term that includes several levels of care and types of programs.

The two levels of care that are most commonly associated with nursing homes are: skilled nursing facility (SNF) care and intermediate care facility (ICF).

Personal Care Facilities

Definition: A living arrangement that provides residents with meals and assistance with bathing, dressing, toileting, and other activities of daily living. With certain exceptions, nursing care is not provided. These may also be referred to as boarding homes.

Telephone Contact/Helpline

Definition: A service that may provide one or all of the following: counseling, information, referral, and check-up services or monitoring of all health-related problems.

Transportation Services

Definition: Provides or arranges for transportation to allow disabled or older adults to meet daily needs and to have access to a broad range of services.

Wellness Programs

Definition: Includes health maintenance, disease prevention and exercise programs for social, psychological, and physical well-being. Examples include risk reduction (e.g., smoking cessation and weight reduction programs); education in health and nutrition; and exercise and stress management programs.

THE LONG-TERM CARE ADMINISTRATOR

The long-term care administrator should have the basic characteristics of any successful manager including skills in planning, organizing, diplomacy, and leadership. Expertise in finance and health care organization is also important. But in addition to these traits, the long-term care administrator has to adapt to the unique aspects of this part of the medical care system and possess the following:

- An understanding of the concept of comprehensive health. In working with geriatric centers, an administrator has a major coordinating role. The administrator must help develop programs for patient placement and discharge where appropriate.
- An understanding of the needs of the aged and chronically ill and the know-how to provide for those needs. Understanding the causes and reasons for chronic illness is the first step in providing an effective program and environment.
- The knowledge that teaching in this environment is important. Working with the aged and chronically ill can be depressing and frustrating. The administrator must be able to establish educational programs to sensitize staff members to the special problems and opportunities in this area.
- A desire to be a change agent. Long-term care is a changing field. There are many opportunities for innovation. The administrator must be bold enough to seek change.

Presently, there are too few well-trained and motivated long-term care administrators. The number of institutions is growing rapidly. If you have the personality for this special administrative work and the ambition to study and grow, long-term care administration could be in your managerial future.

CHAPTER 7

EDUCATIONAL PREPARATION

An effective health administrator performs basic management functions such as assisting in managing policy, managing personnel and materials, and establishing and monitoring budgets. Most administrators are also involved in public relations activities.

In days past, administrators were frequently secured from other professional ranks. In fact, many administrators were former nursing administrators, physicians, and accountants. Yet because of the variety of activities and departments an administrator is responsible for today, a specialized educational background is required for the job. Based on a recent survey of members of the College of Healthcare Executives 84% hold master's degrees, while 11% hold only a bachelor's degree.

FORMAL TRAINING

Over the last twenty-five years, the number of individuals who have been specifically educated in university-based health administration programs has grown significantly. Approximately 1,600 master's and 800 baccalaureate-level health care managers graduate from these programs each year. Of these graduates, approximately fifty percent are women. In addition, university graduate programs in the United States have continued to increase over the years. The majority of these programs are located in schools of business. Other programs are found in schools of public health and also in selected interdisciplinary settings.

It is the master's degree that is most widely accepted as the required academic preparation for health administration. Many of these programs offer full- and part-time study so that students can both work in their current positions and continue to grow professionally by attending school.

Many of the master's degree programs have as part of their curriculum some type of an internship or residency. During this time students in the master's degree program go into a health care organization for a period of many weeks or months to learn and work. A much briefer period may be called a clerkship. During residency, students spending time in hospitals rotate through various departments of the hospital. In recent years, many of the programs have de-emphasized practical experience and substituted on-campus academic programs. Many students go directly from undergraduate school into the master's degree program; however, schools do still look with favor on individuals who have had practical experience in the health care field.

Many master's programs are based in a business administration school and offer a master of business administration degree (MBA) with a concentration in health administration. Some programs offer the master of public administration (MPA) and still others have their program in health care administration based in the public health school and offer a master of public health. Still other programs offer a master of science in health administration, and some a master in hospital administration.

THE GRADUATE CURRICULUM PROGRAMS

University graduate education involves two areas: 1) the fundamental management/administrative coursework; and 2) practical "hands-on" experience such as management research projects and clerkships. This would include the residency.

The coursework is focused mainly on management skill requirements relevant to the health industry such as organization behavior, quantitative methods, finance, information systems, law, strategic planning, policy development, marketing, personnel management, and labor relations. Knowledge of social, ethical, political, economic, and legal forces that influence the development of organizations is necessary for successful performance in this field. An understanding of areas such as social and behavioral disciplines, individual, social, and environmental health, and disease control is also desirable.

As a general rule, graduate programs in health administration cover three principal learning areas. One area covered in most programs is management theory. This includes traditional management principles as well as health care administrative theory and organization. This area also covers financial management, economics, human relations, and the behavioral sciences. The second learning area covered in most programs deals with the health and medical care system. Included in this topic is a detailed explanation of health care organizations and their function. Also covered are the issues that affect the system, including environmental and personal health characteristics. Planning and economic considerations in the health care system are also covered under this topic. Third, programs cover more specific issues related to hospitals, health institutions, and more general health care issues. In this area the role of health care institutions and providers within the health care system are examined. Also the specifics of managing health care finances, personnel, and resources are covered under this category, including study of the medical staff and quality care issues.

No matter in which school a graduate program is offered, most require the equivalent of at least two full years of study. Some schools will offer in addition to, or as part of the two years, certain types of field work. This is usually known as an administrative residency, and is conducted under the supervision of a practicing administrator.

UNDERGRADUATE PROGRAMS

The development of undergraduate health care administration programs is a relatively new occurrence. It was not until the early 1970s that full-fledged undergraduate programs with well-trained, full-time faculty began to operate. To date there is a wide variety of undergraduate programs, and this, coupled with their newness, makes it difficult to speculate what this degree will mean to the profession in the future. Up to this time, the number of graduates has been small.

Though there are differences in each of the programs, most seem to be focused on preparing managers for less complex institutions than hospitals. For example, they concentrate on preparing students to be administrators of nursing homes, clinics, and group practices, as well as managers of hospital departments.

SELECTING AN EDUCATIONAL PROGRAM

Students should research a variety of schools before finally selecting one. If they do, they will be faced with comparing perhaps several different programs. Which program is best for you and how do you go about determining this? There are a variety of factors to be considered. The following is a list of items to weigh:

- tuition and other costs in the program;
- class size and the ratio of faculty to students;
- the percentage of full-time versus part-time faculty;
- the amount of research and publishing done by the faculty;

**Active* Members of the American College of Healthcare Executives
by Educational Degree and District (Percent)**

	1	2	3	4	5	6	7	8	9	
	New England & East Canada	*Mid-Atlantic*	*Southeast*	*East Northern Central*	*West Northern Central & Mid-Canada*	*Southern Central/ South West*	*West & Western Canada*	*Uni-formed Services*	*Foreign Non-Canadian*	*Total*
Degree										
Doctorate	5.2	5.2	4.3	4.8	5.2	5.0	6.1	2.8	8.9	4.9
Masters	85.9	84.5	83.4	86.4	83.0	81.1	85.1	76.6	78.2	83.6
Bachelors	8.4	10.1	11.6	8.3	10.8	13.2	8.6	20.2	12.1	11.0
Other**	0.5	0.2	0.6	0.5	0.8	0.5	0.2	0.4	0.4	0.4
None	0.0	0.0	0.1	0.0	0.2	0.2	0.0	0.0	0.4	0.1
Total	100.0%	100.0%	100.0%	100.0%	100.0%	100.0%	100.0%	100.0%	100.0%	100.0%
Number	2,392	3,540	4,492	2,795	1,854	2,168	2,432	1,737	257	21,667

*Excludes student associates, candidates for associate, faculty associates, and life-status members.

**Includes associate arts, certificates, and diplomas awarded from junior college, vocational, and professional postsecondary programs.

Active* Members by Educational Field and District (Percent)

	1	2	3	4	5	6	7	8	9	
	New England & East Canada	*Mid-Atlantic*	*Southeast*	*East Northern Central*	*West Northern Central & Mid-Canada*	*Southern Central/ South West*	*West & Western Canada*	*Uni-formed Services*	*Foreign Non-Canadian*	*Total*
Field										
Hospital/ Health Adminis-tration	54.8	54.6	55.2	53.9	60.2	56.5	54.4	45.3	52.5	54.5
Business	21.7	23.3	24.0	25.0	21.2	23.5	22.1	29.2	22.0	23.7
Public Health/ Public Adminis-tration	4.7	3.2	2.9	2.3	2.1	1.6	5.0	5.1	5.5	3.3
Other	18.8	18.9	17.9	18.8	16.5	18.4	18.5	20.4	20.0	18.5
Total	100.0%	100.0%	100.0%	100.0%	100.0%	100.0%	100.0%	100.0%	100.0%	100.0%
Number	2,378	3,512	4,444	2,767	1,842	2,151	2,404	1,723	255	21,476

*Excludes student associates, candidates for associate, faculty associates, and life-status members.

- the core curriculum, i.e., business, public administration, or public health;
- the program's job placement service;
- the length of time for field experience (clerkships, internships, or residencies).

As of today, unlike many other health care professions, a license is really not required to work in health care administration. This is not true in every administrative area, however. For example, all states and the District of Columbia require nursing home administrators to be licensed. Yet licensing may not be directly related to a master's degree program. Generally the states, though not uniformly, require a specified level of education, such as a bachelor's degree, plus some degree of experience in the field.

Postgraduate Training and Continuing Education

Two types of postgraduate training opportunities include the fellowship program, which is usually one to two years, and the management development program, which is one to four years.

A fellowship is a program that provides practical experience in a health care setting after receiving a master's degree. Some health care settings include university teaching hospital/medical schools, hospitals, managed care organizations, insurance companies, multi-institutional organizations, foundations, and associations. A list of fellowship opportunities is available free of charge from the American College of Healthcare Executives called the "Directory of Postgraduate Fellowships and Management Development Programs." It is an up-to-date listing of postgraduate fellowships and management programs in the United States, Canada, and other international settings.

Learning is a life-long experience. The professional administrator should not be satisfied with having earned an undergraduate or graduate degree. It is incumbent upon modern health care managers to continue their education through formal continuing education programs. The American College of Healthcare Executives offers some of the very finest comprehensive continuing educational opportunities and professional development programs for its members. Its programs include seminars on problem-solving, on the development of management skills, and on a variety of other pertinent subjects essential for the dedicated health care manager. As in so many professions, it is important for top people in the field to stay up-to-date on contemporary developments. Individuals going into health administration must be prepared to continue to keep up-to-date by reading regularly the professional periodicals and journals that are available through the American College of Healthcare Executives and other professional associations. A list of professional associations and selected journals is provided in Appendix A.

The master's degree continues to be the most widely recognized means of preparing for a career in health administration. This is because of the success over the past decades of the men and women who, holding master's degrees, have accomplished so much in the management of health care institutions and systems. Because the field is changing and rapidly expanding, there will continue to be a demand for well-trained administrators.

CHAPTER 8

WHAT ADMINISTRATORS DO

Many of today's health care institutions and organizations must be in top running order night and day. In those institutions the staff must be thoroughly trained and the facility ready for any emergency that might arise. Though hospitals and other provider institutions are primarily concerned with the sick, they are also businesses and must be operated efficiently. It is the administrator who is held accountable for managing the hospital. Such a formidable task requires certain skills.

NECESSARY SKILLS

A profile of a successful health care administrator indicates that he or she must have a mixed array of technical and professional business skills. The basic skill requirements for a health administrator parallel those required for most executive management jobs, but there is the added responsibility of understanding health care systems. The health administrator must be able to manage people, finances, and material. The modern manager must be both creative and cost effective. An accomplished administrator must have three basic types of skills: technical, human relations, and conceptual.

Technical Skills

The health care administrator must be proficient in specific types of business methods, procedures, and techniques in addition to possessing specialized knowledge of analytical tools. Administrators are required to run a modern-day health care institution. Obviously, such job responsibilities require that the administrator be a good organizer. Within the hospital, for example, there are physicians comprising a medical staff and perhaps hundreds of other employees who must be effectively organized. Further, there is a need to understand and develop systems. Frequently the administrator must formulate rules and regulations which govern the hospital. Administrators should have a working knowledge of personnel and business administration and an understanding of the role of public relations in the institution. Expertise in planning has become more important as hospitals have grown. Also an understanding of financial management and reimbursement systems is absolutely necessary to keep the institution fiscally solvent.

Human Relations Skills

The administrator must be able to work effectively as a team member and be able to promote cooperation among the other members of management. The successful administrator has to possess very sharp human relations skills and the ability to work with tact and diplomacy. This is especially important since administrators deal frequently with a variety of people including doctors, nurses, engineers, accountants, patients, and visitors. The successful administrator must produce an aura of satisfaction for the complaining patient, relative, or employee. The stage of cooperation in dealing with employees and medical staff is set by the administrator. This requires tact, diplomacy, and seriousness. A sense of humor is also important. Perhaps the most important skill is the ability to work with people. The administrator will find varied, difficult problems to solve among groups including, but not limited to, the board of trustees, the medical staff, patients, and assorted personnel. Problems must be resolved in order for the hospital or health care institution to operate effectively. As in any business, being an accurate judge of human nature is a valuable asset.

Conceptual Skills

The administrator must be able to see the institution in a broad perspective. Where the institution fits into the community must be understood, and the institution's contribution to the economy of the community must be appreciated. Administrators must understand the political, social, and economic forces that affect the institution. With this understanding and sensitivity, the administrator is expected to lead the hospital or health care institution as well as be a leader within the community at large. Successful administrators agree that the ability to judge human nature is critical to effective leadership. The administrator must understand broad health issues and then offer a vision of how to cope with them to the institution.

The combination of technical, human relations, and conceptual skills required to be a successful administrator is important today in managing varied, complex health care institutions.

New Administrative Skills

Since hospitals are so dynamic and are changing so rapidly, new skills are always in demand. Customer (patient) orientation, an entrepreneurial spirit, adaptive skills, and good instincts are some of the new skills needed. Elements of customer orientation include guest relations programs, local business and industry programs, and the physician's role. Since the majority of patients are directed to the hospital by physicians, the institution they choose is the one that creates an atmosphere that makes their lives rewarding, pleasant, and satisfying. Administrators who support customer orientation are invariably successful. Also key to being a successful administrator is an entrepreneurial spirit. Those administrators who do best are those who, using their instincts, aggressively seek new ways of improving their hospital and gaining a competitive advantage. Successful administrators, in order to survive and prosper in an uncertain and competitive world, are continually adjusting their management style to adapt to the environment.

Effective Leadership—Putting the Skills Together

Health care organizations are undergoing unprecedented change. At this time it is more critical than ever for managers to know where the organization is headed, the vision for the organization. What is needed from today's health care manager is effective leadership. What does it take to be a successful leader in health care administration? Success in leadership requires risk taking, imagination, and a willingness to trust and engender trust. Especially important in health care management is the ability to work within and motivate teams of people. Effective leadership means pulling together and motivating team play and team success. Effective managers are not a "solo dog act." Often it is the leader's task to select the best people and then turn them loose.

ACTIVITIES AND TASKS

Health care administrators perform a variety of tasks and functions, and quite naturally these vary with their institution and specific job assignment within that institution. The senior administrators in hospitals and other health care institutions are referred to as the chief executive officers. The other managers and assistant administrators within the organization must work with and support the chief executive officer's objectives and goals. This is called "team play" and is critical in health care management. It is important to understand how the chief executive officers operate and what they do in the course of a day's work.

The hospital administrator of the 1950s and 1960s was primarily concerned with the internal operations of the hospital (the planning, organizing, supervising, and controlling of the hospital's operations). This frequently involved bargaining with employees and determining the best systems and methods to internally manage the institution. However, in the 1970s, 1980s, and into the 1990s, major changes overtook the hospital as well as the medical care system. It was during this period that the administrator started to assume dual responsibilities inside and outside the hospital. The chief executive officer has become more involved in activities outside the institution. Today the modern health care executive must strike the proper balance between outside institutional activities and inside activities.

Inside Activities

Traditionally, it has been the hospital administrator's job to see that the hospital's buildings and facilities are in adequate running order and that the employees are qualified for their specific jobs. In fact, legally it is the administrator who must answer for the acts of the employees under his or her supervision. Another traditional function of the hospital administrator is to deal with the physicians on the medical staff. The administrator has the responsibility of keeping the physicians informed about the important happenings in the hospital and its plans. Further, the administrator traditionally has had the responsibility of keeping the hospital's governing body, the board of trustees, informed.

Generally the administrator must attend board meetings in order to communicate ideas, thoughts, and policies that will help the hospital. Financial management is a traditional responsibility for administrators too. They prepare and defend annual budgets to be approved by the board of trustees. This includes identifying new services that need to be offered as well as new equipment that needs to be purchased. Negotiating reimbursement rates and contracts with managed care organizations and preparing monthly financial statements and statistical data that are presented to the board are among the internal tasks performed by an administrator.

The inside activities can be grouped under duties that include the review and establishment of hospital policies and procedures, supervision of the hospital and its operations, and dealings with employees. The administrator must establish the proper working conditions and environment for employees and see that the morale of the staff is maintained at a high level. Finally, the administrator is responsible for ensuring that the hospital is well furnished with the supplies and equipment required to treat patients. Additionally, the administrator must make sure that the building is maintained in safe operating condition and that adequate sanitary conditions exist.

Outside Activities

The outside activities of today's administrator are numerous. They include relating to the community, understanding governmental relationships, and participating in outside educational opportunities and joint planning activities with other health care providers. One of the roles of the modern administrator is to educate the community about hospital operations and health care matters. Frequently this is done through publishing brochures and pamphlets or speaking to community groups. It is the administrator's responsibility to present a positive image of the hospital. Public relations duties are considered key outside activities, and the administrator must encourage an understanding of the hospital's programs by using the mass media. One of the most valuable accomplishments of today's administrator is the negotiating of contracts with third-party payers (insurance companies) who pay for the patients' bills. This is a time-consuming activity requiring a combination of management and negotiating skills.

Modern hospital administrators direct and coordinate the activities of their institutions. They take on the role of promoting favorable public relations not only within the community but also among the hospital employees and staff. Administrators must see that the hospital continually updates its buildings and equipment. They also must coordinate the activities of a variety of personnel and groups, including the medical staff and the board of trustees.

HOW ADMINISTRATORS SPEND THEIR TIME

Today's hospital executives spend their time on a wide range of activities. Responsibilities involve planning, controlling, organizing, directing and coordinating, operating, and extramural activities. The specific nature of these responsibilities includes health industry activities, administrative education, public and community relations, systems, financial and business management, physical facilities and equipment oversight, team management, meetings, policy formulation and implementation, personnel management, legal and governmental, clinical service operation, administrative research, and medical center operation. All of these functions could make up the typical day of a hospital executive.

The Nature of an Administrator's Activities in a Hospital

ACTIVITIES	PERCENT OF TIME
Departmental operation	10.8
Health industry activities	29.9
Administrative education	10.5
Public and community relations	2.8
Systems	1.9
Financial and business management	6.3
Physical facilities and equipment	4.5
Group administrative meeting	8.2
Policy formulation and implementation	9.5
Personnel management	1.0
Legal and governmental	1.6
Clinical service operation	4.1
Administrative research	4.5
Other	2.1
Hospital operation	2.3

Source: Hospital, J.A.H.A.

Nature of Work

As you can see, the administrator's job is not an eight-hour, nine-to-five position. Because the administrator is concerned with all phases of the hospital's operations, he or she is frequently out of the office keeping track of hospital activities. Frequent visits must be made to the various hospital departments. And since the administrator is called upon to be the institution's representative to the public, he or she may be found addressing various civic or fraternal groups. Energy, good health, and vitality are essential to someone in this position. Because much of the administrator's work involves dealing with people and showing patience, an even temper is also a valuable asset to him or her.

ADVANCEMENT IN THE FIELD

It should be clear by now that it is very unlikely that a graduate directly out of college or even recently out of a graduate program in health care administration will move immediately into the chief executive officer's job in a hospital. Administrators advance in the profession by gaining experience in management activities and building a successful record of accomplishment. This is commonly done by taking jobs in a hospital that offer experience in one or more areas of specialized administration, for example, working as a department head in charge of purchasing or personnel. Beginners should gain experience in budgeting, handling employees, supervision, and reimbursement systems. After building a track record at lower-level management positions, the administrator will generally seek promotion to successively more responsible positions, perhaps as an administrative assistant, then assistant or associate administrator. In some instances administrators begin their careers outside the hospital field proper and then enter at a top-level management position, but this is not very common. Eventually, regardless of the specific career path, most administrators hope to be the chief executive officer of their organization.

CHAPTER 9

GETTING STARTED AND YOUR FUTURE

JOB SOURCES

When you are seeking a position in health administration, remember that you are not only competing against your peers— you are also competing against yourself. The more you do to advance your job-hunting skills now, the better equipped you will be to face the challenge of the future. Two channels exist for job searches, published and unpublished sources. First let's discuss the method that is used most often.

Statistics prove that three-fourths of all job candidates in the health administration market secure their positions through personal contacts. Offhand you may be thinking that you are a member of the remaining quarter of applicants who must use other innovative measures to locate a job. This is not necessarily so. If you examine your own personal contacts (referred to as your network) you may be surprised to learn how many of them can be influential in your benefit.

NETWORKING IS THE KEY TO SUCCESS

Here is how to go about this process.

Draw up a network identification form by listing four main headings across the top of a piece of paper. These will be professional colleagues, academic associations, friends, acquaintances, and relatives. (See Network Identification Form). Systematically fill in the columns with names of people who might be able to help you, no matter how remote the chances may seem at present. You may be surprised at the number of people with power who are at your fingertips. Do not hesitate to ask those contacts to help guide you in your employment search. Remember, it means a great deal to speak directly with hospital administrators, assistant administrators, personnel directors, public relations directors, or any influential member of the hospital or institution you might want to join. Such people may be in your network.

Several other job sources are available to you. Let's take a look at the remaining twenty percent of the jobs given to job searchers every year. These jobs are obtained usually through published sources. Many of the graduate programs in hospital administration have alumni bulletins which have handy references to job sources. Try to get in touch with these associations and obtain these publications. You could also utilize your state and local health care associations. Frequently they know about jobs. Also there are local newspapers. Looking at these sources is a routine you should get into. Without a doubt, however, the Sunday *New York Times* and the *Wall Street Journal* are two excellent newspapers carrying health care administration openings. Other sources, especially professional journals, that you should review regularly include: *Hospitals, Modern Healthcare, Hospital Financial Management,* and the *American Journal of Public Health.* Refer to Appendix A of this book for a selected list of the health care journals that often carry job listings.

Network Identification Form

Professional Colleagues	Academic Associations	Friends and Acquaintances	Relatives

PREPARING YOUR RESUME

Chances are your resume will introduce you to your prospective employer. Because this first impression is so important, let us spend some time showing you how to present yourself attractively on paper. It is up to you to tell the prospective employer why he or she should hire you based on the following information: who you are; what you know; what you have done; and what you would like to do for the new employer. When creating your resume, keep in mind that you must be able to support its contents. You may be requested to exemplify your statements during a personal interview. Should this occur, you would be expected to add details without hesitation. Failure to do so would cost you the interview and the job.

The two most popular resume styles that are used regularly by people in health administration are the functional and the accomplishment resumes. Both types contain all the standard autobiographical data, such as your name, address, telephone number, education history, and work experiences. They differ in their approach to employment description.

The functional resume can be advantageous to people with considerable field experience or to those who are just embarking upon the health care area after being employed in another field for a number of years. The functional resume features specific jobs a person has held with minimal supplemental information about accomplishments in that job. For example, you might find the following in a functional resume:

1990 to present: Community Hospital, Charlottesville, N.C. Assistant controller in 200-bed hospital. Reported directly to the controller. Responsible for supervision of fourteen people and a budget of $750,000.

In contrast to the functional resume, the accomplishment resume places considerable emphasis upon the applicant's achievements. A typical resume might include the following:

1992 to present. Assistant Financial Manager. Reorganized a department of fifteen people with the result of increasing productivity by 40% and decreasing cost by 15%.

This type of resume is more interesting to the employer because actual achievements are listed. By listing your accomplishments in specifics, you clearly spell out what you have done in the past and indicate what you are capable of achieving in the future.

Now let us review some of the basic guidelines for developing an effective resume and place these tips into the "Do's and Don'ts" of preparing a resume.

Do's of preparing a resume.

- Start a permanent resume file.
- List all your education experience and achievements.
- Know the kind of work you are seeking.
- Be sure to place your name, address, and telephone number at the top of the resume.
- Give personal information at the end of the resume.
- Be specific.
- Be quantitative.
- Use action words.
- Keep it short (one or two pages).
- Use good bond, white or off-white paper.
- Write a cover letter on the same bond paper.
- Check and recheck for typing errors and misspellings.

Don'ts of preparing a resume.

- Don't include job requirements.
- Don't discuss lack of employment.
- Don't discuss reasons for leaving your present job.
- Don't use gimmicks.
- Don't criticize your former employers.
- Don't include a photograph of yourself.

• Don't use the word *I*.
• Don't use abbreviations.

THE COVER LETTER

Every time you send a resume to a potential employer you must include a cover letter. Often it is this letter that decides whether or not you will be granted an interview. The cover letter must be tailored so you will have the competitive edge over other applicants. If you have trouble writing letters get someone who can write persuasively to aid you in this undertaking.

Let us suppose that you have applied for a position as an administrative assistant at a local hospital. About a hundred other people have also applied. Somehow you have to stand apart from the crowd at the outset. You have to grab the employer's attention by using a degree of flair. Your cover letter introduces you to the employer and hopefully arrests his or her attention, stimulates interest in you, and convinces the employer that you are the person he or she most wants to interview.

Let us spend some time reviewing the basic elements of a cover letter. First make sure that your name, complete address, telephone number, and the date are in the upper right-hand corner of your cover letter. Do not forget to include your area code, especially if you are applying for a position outside of your local area code. If you are employed at present include your business office telephone for initial contact. However, you might want to list a special time when you can be reached at home, such as between the hours of 7 and 9 P.M. The idea is to make it as easy as possible for the employer to contact you. When an employer can choose from over a hundred applications for the same job, it is doubtful that much time will be spent trying to figure out a way to reach a potential applicant.

Next, address the person to whom you are writing by name if possible. Sometimes you will know the person's name and other times it will not be listed in the ad. Therefore, you may have to use your network if you are to write a personal letter. You could also call the hospital or the organization and request the names of the personnel director or the administrator. Remember, you must gain a favorable impression from the start.

What should you include in the body of the cover letter? This depends on why you are writing a letter in the first place. For example, if you were referred by a friend or a colleague from your network you could be writing an unsolicited letter that announces your availability, or you could be answering a publicized job opening. No matter what your reason is, the first thing you must do is establish for the reader exactly why you are writing. In the first sentence you might want to say something like "I am writing you in response to your advertisement for an administrative assistant that was published in *The Philadelphia Inquirer,* July 14."

SUCCESSFUL INTERVIEWING

By now you should be ready for the climax of your job campaign—the interview. You have already realistically assessed your goals, utilizing the network; designed an attractive resume; and written a dynamic cover letter.

If your interview experience is limited or nonexistent, you are probably uncertain or hesitant about what to say or how to say it. To gain practice you can participate in role-playing exercises. Ask a friend to engage in a mock interview session with you.

Most interviewers use a question and answer format. Your task is to respond quickly and intelligently. Chances are you will be asked a few personal questions to break the ice. It is safe to assume you will be asked some of these questions: What do you know about our hospital or institution? What can I do for you? What do you consider your strongest management skill? Why do you want to join our staff? What will you be doing in five years and ten years? What can you tell me about yourself?

If you are being interviewed on a one-to-one basis you will have to handle some things differently that if you are interviewed before a group. As the administrator or the personnel director talks to you, be sure to take notes. Most administrators or people interviewing you feel that note taking signifies an organized, interested applicant.

Now let's review some of the important elements in handling the interview:

- Practice beforehand.
- Be yourself, not an actor.
- Bring extra copies of your resume.
- Study your resume beforehand.
- Tell the interviewers what you can do for them.
- Know and be prepared to discuss three or four of your strongest assets.
- Don't end on a flat negative.
- Don't waste precious time discussing your hobbies.
- Be specific and to the point.
- Keep to the facts, minimize opinions.
- Never argue with the interviewer.
- Be a good listener.
- Take notes.

FOLLOW-UP AND ACCEPTING THE JOB

The first thing you want to do when you leave the interview, whether it was with the administrator or the personnel director, is review the notes you took. Even though you may not have been able to jot down everything you wanted to, take the time now to add any important notes which were omitted earlier. For example, if the administrator confided in you that he or she is having a terrible time trying to find a director of nurses who will produce dynamic results, make sure you not only include this tip, but underline it for emphasis. You can capitalize on the situation. Note taking is *very* important.

You may not always be told why you were rejected by an employer. If this happens you should contact the administrator or personnel director and ask why you are no longer in the running. While this may seem like a painful procedure, you need to make every effort to find out exactly what the reasons were for your elimination. What if you lost the job because of insufficient technical knowledge? If you do not find this out at the start of your job campaign, you can be destroyed in interview after interview. You must be able to correct this gap in your knowledge. Otherwise you will never win a responsible position in health administration.

DOING WELL IN YOUR FIRST JOB

Once you have been selected for a position and have negotiated a fair salary, it is time to start work. Now the question is how do you make a success of your job in health administration? Success is not just getting your position—it is doing well in that position and eventually getting promoted.

There are several things that working administrators should do if they want to be a success. The manager should strive to build a results-oriented track record. This may be the most important advice to the novice manager. Take your job seriously, attack projects with hard work and imagination, and get results.

Administrators must continually develop their communication and public relations skills and quantitative skills. Working on your weak areas serves to continually upgrade your competency as an administrator. Administrators must continue their training and development after their formal schooling. Setting aside time to read professional journals and attending educational seminars and conferences are excellent ways to keep up-to-date and to improve your job skills.

You should know the formal process of how you will be evaluated on the job and specifically what criteria will be used. As a manager, you should know what your boss expects of you. Remember there is also an informal process of performance review. Do not count only on the formal system—be a top-notch performer at all times. You should ask your boss for feedback on your performance. It is your obligation to ask for it—and your boss's obligation to give you a review of your performance.

Try to be a likeable person and set up alliances among your managerial peers. This is very much a part of establishing a job network which will assist you in future promotions. Managers should recognize the two "A" principles—ability and affability. There is no sense in creating ill will in your job. Respect for fellow employees is important.

If you do well in your job, you will undoubtedly be very busy. Administrators must learn to delegate. By delegating you will also be developing your responsibility to others. This is important for your own development also. There may come a time that your boss may consider promoting you. One consideration will be who is capable of taking your position. Training an adequate replacement may allow you to be promoted within the same institution. A competent assistant will also permit you to leave your job from time to time to attend educational programs. If you achieve results and are a top-notch performer, the time will come when you will be asked to move up to a position of greater responsibility. If the new job is in another institution, you should leave your present position in the best of circumstances. Don't "muddy the waters" just because you have a new job. Leave with good relations on your own timetable.

THE OUTLOOK FOR JOBS

What will health care and health care management look like in the year 2000? Where there is change, there is opportunity. For example, there is a major shift from individual hospitals to multi-hospital and integrated delivery systems (IDS) and hospitals growing together. This has created new jobs at a corporate level. It is also believed that the development of these multihospital systems will increase the need for specialty managers.

Health Care Trends

- What will healthcare look like in the year 2000? Inpatient hospital days may decrease 15% to 25% while outpatient procedures will increase 20% to 30%. Total hospital revenue will be almost equally divided between in- and outpatient services. However, it is likely to shrink 8% to 12% over the next five years. By the year 2000 some 800 regional integrated healthcare delivery networks will account for 80% of all healthcare delivered. ("Transition to outpatient care accelerates," *MedPro Month,* vol. 5, #8, August 1995, pg. 140)
- A look at the demographics of our country shows that the sixty-five-and-older group is growing significantly. Herein lies the need for long-term health care management.
- In health care there is a great need for experienced health care management consultants.
- The growing complexity in the health field brings with it more national associations and professional societies, as well as more agencies regulating the quality of care and credentialling

associations. Add to this the increase in the number of educational programs. All of these changes will create new jobs
and positions for health care managers.
- There will be managed care organizations (MCOs). There are
currently 478 HMOs and 620 PPOs in operation, and the federal authorities expect these numbers to continue to increase.
As in many growth industries, there will be a demand for
qualified administrators. Many group practices require
administrators or business managers to assist them in their
practice. Similar to the hospital administrator, these administrators must be familiar with finances, patient accounts, handling records and procedures, personnel, and matters related
to the medical staff. Other fast-growing alternative delivery
systems include freestanding surgi-centers, urgi-centers, can-
cer centers, and imaging centers. Where there is such rapid
change, there is opportunity for health care managers.

It is clear that competition is keen in health administration. As
new graduates enter the field, they may have to lower their sights
from administrator or assistant administrator positions to middle-
management openings. But perhaps the most important item for a
new graduate to remember is that it is important to gain experience in the health care area. Build a track record, develop managerial skills, stay adaptable and have a thirst of growth, and the new
career opportunities will open up for you.

DIVERSITY IN HEALTH ADMINISTRATION

America's health care labor force in the twenty-first century
will be culturally diverse. Many publications and experts have dis-
cussed the future trends for the changing workplace. For example,
nearly two-thirds of the new entrants by the year 2000 will be
women and by that same year, 61% of all women of working age
are expected to have jobs.

Many years ago it was common to see women as hospital administrators. Though at that time they may not have been called administrators, they did in effect run the hospital. In those days administrators were usually nurses or nuns who were in charge of religious institutions. However, a review of recent history shows that administration has been a male-dominated profession, though this is changing.

Distribution of Gender within Senior Administrative Positions

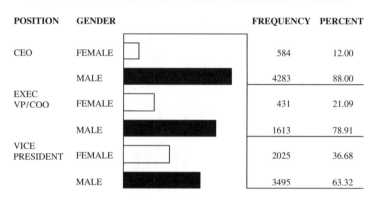

POSITION	GENDER		FREQUENCY	PERCENT
CEO	FEMALE		584	12.00
	MALE		4283	88.00
EXEC VP/COO	FEMALE		431	21.09
	MALE		1613	78.91
VICE PRESIDENT	FEMALE		2025	36.68
	MALE		3495	63.32

Data represents active ACHE members as of January 1, 1995.

Educators are quite enthusiastic about the number of female students going into health administration programs, since their academic quality and commitment is very high. Though women do face different challenges in becoming CEOs, there is no doubt that women are competing successfully with their male counterparts. The bulk of male administrators do deal with the women in their ranks on a professional basis, showing no discrimination or favors. This is what women managers need and should demand. Success for women will come at all levels in health administration.

PROFESSIONAL SOCIETIES AND SELECTED JOURNALS

PROFESSIONAL SOCIETY MEMBERSHIP

American Academy of Medical Administrators
30555 Southfield Road
President's Office
Suite 150
Southfield. Michigan 48076–7747
810-540-4310
FAX: 810-645-0590

The American Academy of Medical Administrators was founded in Boston, Massachusetts in 1957 and today has a membership of over 4,000 health care professionals in the U.S., Canada, the Caribbean, and other countries. The mission of the AAMA, a not-for-profit association of health care professionals, is to develop and refine concepts and practices in the field of health care administration and to promote the advancement of its members in knowledge, professional development, credentialing, and personal achievements through continuing education and research in health care management.

In recent years, the Academy has developed new and innovative approaches in fulfilling its commitment to all levels of management within health administration through the founding of new chapter organizations. These organizations have been formed to assist professional managers in special areas such as cardiology, oncology, information systems, home health, and neuromusculoskeletal areas.

American College of Healthcare Executives
    One North Franklin Street
    President's Office
    Suite 1700
    Chicago, Illinois 60606–3491
    312-424-2800
    FAX: 312-424-0023
    World Wide Web Address: HTTP://www.ACHE.org

The American College of Healthcare Executives (ACHE) is an international professional society of more than 30,000 health care executives. The College is known for its prestigious credentialing and educational programs. ACHE's annual Congress on Healthcare Management draws more than 4,000 participants each year. The College is also known for its journal, *Hospital and Health Services Administration,* and its magazine, *Healthcare Executive,* as well as ground-breaking research and career development and public policy programs. Through such efforts, the College works toward its goal of improving the health status of society by advancing health care management excellence.

American College of Health Care Administrators
    325 South Patrick Street
    President's Office
    Alexandria, Virginia 22314–3571
    703-739-7900
    FAX: 703-739-7901

The American College of Health Care Administrators (ACHCA) is a professional society of administrators of long-term health programs primarily serving the aged and chronically ill. Founded in 1962 as the American College of Nursing Home Administrators, ACHCA is the only organization representing solely the professional long-term care administrator.

ACHCA is dedicated to the professional advancement of the long-term care health administrator through education, research, informational services, professional representation, and leadership. The college has over 6,400 members in the United States and Canada.

American College of Physician Executives
4890 West Kennedy Boulevard
Executive Vice-President
Suite 200
Tampa, Florida 33609–2575
813-287-2000
FAX: 813-287-8993
World Wide Web Address: HTTP://www.ACPE.org

The American College of Physician Executives (ACPE), formerly the American Academy of Medical Directors, was founded in 1975 and is the only national professional and educational association exclusively for physicians in positions of organizational leadership throughout the United States.

The ACPE is recognized by the American Medical Association as the national specialty society representing medical management. It currently serves over 10,000 physicians who hold positions of medical director, chief executive officer, vice president of medical affairs, dean, chief of staff, and chief of service in hospitals, group practices, managed care organizations, universities, industry, insurance, and government.

American Public Health Association
1015 Fifteenth Street, N.W.
Executive Director
Washington, D.C. 20005
202-789-5600
FAX: 202-789-5661
World Wide Web Address: HTTP://www.APHA.org

Established in 1872, the American Public Health Association (APHA) is devoted to the universal protection and promotion of public health and the equality of health services for all persons.

The APHA achieves these goals by: (1) setting standards for alleviating health problems, (2) initiating projects designed for improving health both nationally and internationally, (3) researching health problems and offering solutions based on that research, (4) launching public awareness campaigns about specific health dangers, (5) publishing numerous materials reflecting the latest findings and developments in public health, and (6) publicizing a year-round schedule of action implementation programs. Throughout its history, APHA has fostered significant advancement in personal health services; improved the environment, training, and credentialing of health professionals; and worked for the prevention of disease.

The membership represents all of the disciplines and specialties in public health. Twenty-four special sections represent the various disciplines and special interest areas within APHA.

Association of Mental Health Administrators
   60 Revere Drive
   Executive Director
   Suite 500
   Northbrook, Illinois 60062
   847-480-9626
   FAX: 847-480-9282
   World Wide Web Address: HTTP://www.AMHA.org

The Association of Mental Health Administrators (AMHA) was formed in 1959 during the annual meeting of the American Psychiatric Association's Hospital and Community Psychiatry Institute. AMHA adopted its current name in the mid-1960s, to reflect rapid changes in the national mental health scene and the inception of the Community Mental Health Centers System. Present AMHA membership represents a broad cross section of the professional managers in mental health, mental retardation, developmental disabilities, and addiction program administration and includes chief executives, state commissioners, and fiscal program and support managers. Every treatment setting is represented. The association constantly seeks to improve the administrative function in all mental health services through continuing education programs for its members and by maximizing formal and informal opportunities for communication and collaboration.

Canadian College of Health Services Executives
    350 Sparks Street
    President's Office
    Suite 402
    Ottawa, Ontario
    Canada K1R 7S8
    613-235-7218
    FAX: 613-235-5451
    World Wide Web Address: HTTP://www.CCHSE.ca

Founded in 1970, the Canadian College of Health Service Executives is a national, professional association which serves the needs of more than 3,000 executives and senior managers from hospitals, long-term care, government, community health, teaching, home care, consulting, and corporate sectors.

The College's mission is to provide leadership in the Canadian health system for excellence in health services management by developing and promoting quality standards, research, certification, and professional development. The College is known for its credential of Certified Health Executive (CHE) and as the publisher of the quarterly journal, *Healthcare Management FORUM.*

Canadian Public Health Association
    1565 Carling Ave., Suite 400
    Executive Director
    Ottawa, Ontario
    Canada K1Z 8Rl
    613-725-3769
    FAX: 613-725-9826
    World Wide Web Address: HTTP://www.CPHA.ca

The Canadian Public Health Association (CPHA) is a national not-for-profit, voluntary association that encourages membership from all health groups and the public. CPHA is associated with ten provincial/territorial public health Branches Associations. CPHA undertakes programs in the areas of public health, health promotion and protection, and health public policy, publishes the *Canadian Journal of Public Health,* and is the sole agent in Canada for World Health Organization publications.

Medical Group Management Association
   104 Inverness Terrace East
   Chief Executive Officer
   Englewood, Colorado 80112–5306
   303-799-1111
   FAX: 303-643-4427
   World Wide Web Address: HTTP://www.MGMA.com

A non-profit corporation founded in 1926, the Medical Group Management Association (MGMA) is the oldest and largest organization in the field of medical group practice. MGMA's 6,800 medical group and 17,000 individual members represent over 137,000 group practice physicians internationally. MGMA's mission is to advance the art and science of medical practice management, to improve the health of our communities. The MGMA has two affiliated organizations, the Center for Research in Ambulatory Health Care Administration that was founded in 1973, and the American College of Medical Practice Executives, founded in 1956.

National Association of Health Services Executives
   8630 Fenton Street
   Association Director
   Suite 328
   Silver Spring, Maryland 20910
   202-628-3953
   FAX: 301-588-0011

The National Association of Health Services Executives (NAHSE) was founded in 1968 in response to a challenge by the late Whitney M. Young, Jr., Executive Director of the National Urban League, who called upon black and other minority health services administrators to become involved in the promotion of quality health services to the poor and disadvantaged citizens of America. Since its founding, NAHSE has become involved in health careers programs, health administration education, health legislation and regulations, and a variety of community service projects. The organization is responsible for the creation of the Summer Work-Study Program (1970) that operated for eight years as a joint program of NAHSE and the Association of University Programs in Health Administration (AUPHA).

Currently, twenty NAHSE chapters exist in locations throughout the country representing approximately 1,100 regular and student members and 30 institutional members. Membership is open to all persons interested in improvement of the quality of health services to minority and disadvantaged populations.

SELECTED JOURNALS

American Journal of Public Health. Published monthly by the American Public Health Association, 1015 Fifteenth Street, NW, Washington, DC 20005.

Contemporary Long-Term Care. Published by Advantage Publishing, Inc., 1801 West End Avenue, Fifth Floor, Nashville, Tennessee 37203–2505.

Health Care Management Review. Published quarterly by Aspen Publishers, Inc., 1600 Research Boulevard, Rockville, Maryland 20850.

Healthcare Financial Management. Published monthly by the Healthcare Financial Management Association, Two Westbrook Corporate Center, Westchester, Illinois 60153. World Wide Web @ HTTP://www. HFMA.org.

Health Progress. Published monthly by the Catholic Health Association of the United States, 4455 Woodsen Road, St. Louis, Missouri 63134.

Hospitals. Published twice a month by the American Hospital Association, 211 East Chicago Avenue, Chicago, Illinois 60611.

Hospital and Health Services Administration. Published quarterly by
   Health Administration Press, 1021 East Huron Street, Ann Arbor,
   Michigan, 48104–9990.
Journal of Long-Term Care Administration. Published quarterly by the
   American College of Healthcare Administrators, 8120 Woodmont
   Avenue, Suite 200, Bethesda, MD 20814.
Medical Group Management. Published bimonthly by the Medical Group
   Management Association, 1355 South Colorado Avenue, Englewood,
   CO 80112.
Modern Healthcare. Published monthly by Crain Communications,
   Incorporated, 740 North Rush Street, Chicago, Illinois 60611. World
   Wide Web @ HTTP://www.modernhealthcare.com.

Source: Health Services Administration Education 1996–1998 Directory
of Programs, The Association of University Programs in Health
Administration (AUPHA), 1911 North Fort Myer Drive, Suite 503,
Arlington, Virginia 22209, (703) 524-5500. (ISBN 0160–4961).
Copyright © 1996 by The Association of University Programs in Health
Administration, Tenth Edition, *Printed in the United States of America.*

APPENDIX B

MASTER'S PROGRAMS IN HEALTH SERVICES ADMINISTRATION

	Program in Health Administration Accredited by ACEHSA	*Program Located in School of Business Accredited by AACSB*	*Program Located in School of Public Health Accredited by CEPH*	*Program Located in School of Medicine Accredited by LCME*	*Program Located in School of Other Specialized Accreditation*
University of Alabama at Birmingham Department of Health Administration	✓				
University of Alberta Graduate Program in Health Services Administration	✓			✓	
Arizona State University Graduate Program in Health Services Administration	✓	✓			

	Program in Health Administration Accredited by ACEHSA	Program Located in School of Business Accredited by AACSB	Program Located in School of Public Health Accredited by CEPH	Program Located in School of Medicine Accredited by LCME	Program Located in School of Other Specialized Accreditation
University of Arkansas at Little Rock Graduate Program in Health Services Administration	✓				
U.S. Army–Baylor University Graduate Program in Health Care Administration	✓				
Boston University Health Care Management Program	✓	✓			
University of California—Berkeley Graduate Program in Health Services Management	✓	✓	✓		
University of California—Los Angeles Program in Health Services Management	✓	✓	✓		
University of Chicago Graduate Program in Health Administration and Policy	✓	✓			✓

	Program in Health Administration Accredited by ACEHSA	Program Located in School of Business Accredited by AACSB	Program Located in School of Public Health Accredited by CEPH	Program Located in School of Medicine Accredited by LCME	Program Located in School of Other Specialized Accreditation
City University of New York/ Baruch College Graduate Program in Health Care Administration	✓	✓			
Clark University/ University of Massachusetts Medical School Master in Health Administration Program	✓	✓		✓	
Cleveland State University Graduate Study in Health Care Administration	✓	✓			
University of Colorado at Denver Program in Health Services Administration	✓	✓			
University of Colorado/ Network for Healthcare Management The Executive Program in Health Administration	✓	✓			

	Program in Health Administration Accredited by ACEHSA	Program Located in School of Business Accredited by AACSB	Program Located in School of Public Health Accredited by CEPH	Program Located in School of Medicine Accredited by LCME	Program Located in School of Other Specialized Accreditation
Cornell University Sloan Program in Health Services Administration	✓				
Dalhousie University Master of Health Services Administration	✓				
Duke University Program in Health Services Management	✓	✓			
University of Florida Graduate Program in Health and Hospital Administration	✓	✓			
Florida International University Program in Health Services Administration	✓				✓
The George Washington University Graduate Program in Health Services Management & Policy	✓	✓			

	Program in Health Administration Accredited by ACEHSA	Program Located in School of Business Accredited by AACSB	Program Located in School of Public Health Accredited by CEPH	Program Located in School of Medicine Accredited by LCME	Program Located in School of Other Specialized Accreditation
Georgia State University Graduate Program in Health Administration	✓	✓			
Governors State University Health Services Administration Program	✓				✓
Hartford Graduate Center Health Care Management Program					
University of Houston— Clear Lake Healthcare Administration Program	✓	✓			
Howard University Graduate Program in Health Services Administration		✓			
Indiana University Graduate Program in Health Administration	✓				✓

	Program in Health Administration Accredited by ACEHSA	Program Located in School of Business Accredited by AACSB	Program Located in School of Public Health Accredited by CEPH	Program Located in School of Medicine Accredited by LCME	Program Located in School of Other Specialized Accreditation
University of Iowa Graduate Program in Hospital and Health Administration	✓			✓	
The Johns Hopkins University MHS in Health Finance and Management	✓		✓		
University of Kansas— Lawrence Graduate Program in Health Services Administration	✓				✓
University of Kentucky Master of Health Administration Program	✓				✓
Medical College of Virginia/VA Commonwealth University Graduate Program in Health Administration	✓				

	Program in Health Administration Accredited by ACEHSA	Program Located in School of Business Accredited by AACSB	Program Located in School of Public Health Accredited by CEPH	Program Located in School of Medicine Accredited by LCME	Program Located in School of Other Specialized Accreditation
Medical College of Virginia/VA Commonwealth University Executive Program in Health Services Administration	✓				
Medical University of South Carolina Master of Health Administration Program	✓				
Meharry Medical College Health Services Administration Program	✓			✓	
The University of Memphis Masters of Health Administration Program					✓
University of Miami Health Administration Program	✓	✓			
University of Michigan Master of Health Management and Policy	✓		✓		

	Program in Health Administration Accredited by ACEHSA	Program Located in School of Business Accredited by AACSB	Program Located in School of Public Health Accredited by CEPH	Program Located in School of Medicine Accredited by LCME	Program Located in School of Other Specialized Accreditation
University of Minnesota Program in Healthcare Administration	✓		✓		
University of Missouri—Columbia Program in Health Services Management	✓			✓	
University of Montreal Master's Program in Health Services Administration	✓			✓	
University of New Hampshire Master of Health Administration Program	✓				
New York University Program in Health Policy and Management	✓				✓
University of North Carolina—Chapel Hill Master's Program in Health Policy Administration	✓		✓		

	Program in Health Administration Accredited by ACEHSA	Program Located in School of Business Accredited by AACSB	Program Located in School of Public Health Accredited by CEPH	Program Located in School of Medicine Accredited by LCME	Program Located in School of Other Specialized Accreditation
Northwestern University Program in Health Services Management	✓	✓			
The Ohio State University Graduate Program in Health Services Management & Policy	✓			✓	
University of Oklahoma Graduate Program in Health Administration			✓		
Oregon State University Health Care Administration Program					
University of Ottawa Master's Program in Health Care Management	✓				
University of Pennsylvania Graduate Program in Health Care Management	✓	✓			

	Program in Health Administration Accredited by ACEHSA	Program Located in School of Business Accredited by AACSB	Program Located in School of Public Health Accredited by CEPH	Program Located in School of Medicine Accredited by LCME	Program Located in School of Other Specialized Accreditation
The Pennsylvania State University Graduate Studies in Health Policy and Administration	✓				
University of Pittsburgh Health Administration Program	✓	✓	✓		
University of Puerto Rico Master in Health Services Administration	✓		✓		
Rush University Graduate Program in Health Systems Management	✓				
Saint Louis University Department of Health Administration	✓		✓		
University of Saint Thomas M.B.A. in Medical Group Management					
San Diego State University Graduate Program in Health Services Administration	✓		✓		

	Program in Health Administration Accredited by ACEHSA	Program Located in School of Business Accredited by AACSB	Program Located in School of Public Health Accredited by CEPH	Program Located in School of Medicine Accredited by LCME	Program Located in School of Other Specialized Accreditation
University of Scranton Graduate Health Administration Program					
Simmons College Graduate Program in Health Care Administration	✓				
University of South Carolina Master of Health Administration Program	✓		✓		
University of South Florida Graduate Program in Health Policy and Management	✓		✓		
University of Southern California Health Services Administration Program	✓				✓
Southwest Texas State University Graduate Program in Health Care Administration	✓				

	Program in Health Administration Accredited by ACEHSA	Program Located in School of Business Accredited by AACSB	Program Located in School of Public Health Accredited by CEPH	Program Located in School of Medicine Accredited by LCME	Program Located in School of Other Specialized Accreditation
Temple University Graduate Program in Health Administration	✓	✓			
Texas Tech University Graduate Program in Health Organization Management	✓	✓			
Texas Woman's University— Houston Center Program in Health Care Administration	✓				
University of Toronto Master of Health Science in Health Administration Program	✓			✓	
Trinity University Graduate Program in Health Care Administration	✓				
Tulane University Master of Health Administration	✓		✓		

	Program in Health Administration Accredited by ACEHSA	Program Located in School of Business Accredited by AACSB	Program Located in School of Public Health Accredited by CEPH	Program Located in School of Medicine Accredited by LCME	Program Located in School of Other Specialized Accreditation
Union College Program in Health Systems Administration	✓				
Washington University Health Administration Program	✓			✓	
University of Washington— Seattle Graduate Program in Health Services Administration	✓		✓		
Widener University Graduate Program in Health and Medical Services Administration	✓				
University of Wisconsin— Madison Administrative Medicine Program		✓		✓	✓
University of Wisconsin— Madison Programs in Health Management		✓		✓	✓

	Program in Health Administration Accredited by ACEHSA	Program Located in School of Business Accredited by AACSB	Program Located in School of Public Health Accredited by CEPH	Program Located in School of Medicine Accredited by LCME	Program Located in School of Other Specialized Accreditation
Xavier University Graduate Program in Health Services Administration	✓				
Yale University Division of Health Policy and Administration	✓		✓	✓	

Source: Health Services Administration Education 1996–1998 Directory of Programs, The Association of University Programs in Health Administration (AUPHA), 1911 North Fort Myer Drive, Suite 503, Arlington, Virginia 22209, (703) 524–5500. (ISBN 0160–4961). Copyright © 1996 by The Association of University Programs in Health Administration, Tenth Edition, *Printed in the United States of America.*

FULL UNDERGRADUATE PROGRAMS IN HEALTH ADMINISTRATION

Alfred University
Program in Health Planning and Management
Ernest Enke, Ph.D., Director

Appalachian State University
Health Care Management Program
Thomas F. McIlwain, Ph.D., Director

California State University—Long Beach
Health Care Administration Program
Harold R. Hunter, Dr.Ph., Director

California State University—Northridge
Health Administration Program
Janet T. Reagan, Ph.D., Director

University of Cincinnati
Program in Health Services Administration
Charles Ellison, Director

University of Connecticut
Center for Health Systems Management
Jeffrey A. Kramer, Ph.D., Director

Eastern Michigan University
Program in Health Administration
Richard L. Douglass, M.P.H., Ph.D., Director

Florida A&M University
Division of Health Care Management
Augustine O. Agho, Ph.D., Program Director

Governors State University
Division of Health Administration
Sang-O Rhee, Ph.D., Division Chair

Idaho State University
Health Care Administration Department
Robert S. Weppner, Ph.D., Chair

University of Illinois at Springfield
Health Services Administration Program
Shahram Heshmat, Ph.D., Director

Ithaca College
Administration of Health Services Program
Carla Wiggins, Chair

University of Kentucky
Division of Health Administration
Joel M. Lee, Dr.P.H., Director

Lehman College/City University of New York
Health Services Administration Program
Ruby Neuhaus, Ph.D., Director

Metropolitan State College of Denver
Department of Nursing and Health Care Management
Robert J. Lander, Director

University of Nevada—Las Vegas
Department of Health Care Administration
David E. Berry, Dr.P.H., Director

University of New Hampshire
Department of Health Management and Policy
James B. Lewis, Sc.D., Director

University of North Carolina—Chapel Hill
Undergraduate Program in Health Policy and Administration
Kerry E. Kilpatrick, Ph.D., Chair

Oregon State University
Health Care Administration Program
Leonard H. Friedman, Ph.D., M.P.H., Program Coordinator

The Pennsylvania State University
Health Policy and Administration Program
Dennis G. Shea, Ph.D., Professor-in-Charge

University of Scranton
Undergraduate Health Administration Program
Alice L. O'Neill, Ed.D., N.H.A., Director

University of South Dakota
Health Services Administration
William T. Reddick, Ph.D., Chair

Southwest Texas State University
Baccalaureate Program in Health Care Administration
Wayne B. Sorensen, Ph.D., FACHE, Chair

Stonehill College
Department of Health Care Administration
Craig S. Higgins, Ph.D., Chair

Tennessee State University/Meharry Medical College
Department of Health Care Administration and Planning
Richard J. Enochs, Dr.P.H., Director

Weber State University
Health Administration Services Program
Phil M. Smith, Ed.D., Director

Western Kentucky University
Health Care Administration Program
Patricia Minors, Ph.D., M.B.A., Program Director

Source: Health Services Administration Education 1996–1998 Directory
of Programs, The Association of University Programs in Health
Administration (AUPHA), 1911 North Fort Myer Drive, Suite 503,
Arlington, Virginia 22209 (703) 524-5500. (ISBN 0160–4961).

SAMPLE JOB ADS

Most job opportunities are published in journals and in newspapers. The job ad is generally either written or directed by the employer. Rather than a detailed job description, the ad reflects in brief form the position requirements and opportunities. In order to reflect the current marketplace, I have compiled a list of contemporary ads that were recently published.

ANATOMY OF AN AD

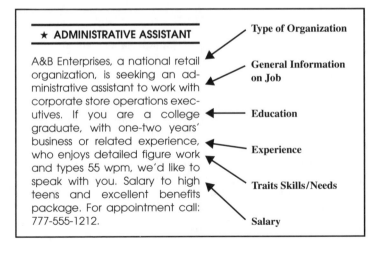

SENIOR ADMINISTRATIVE STAFF

CEO—Large Hospital

President/CEO

One of the nation's premier public, tertiary, teaching medical systems, affiliated with the University is recruiting qualified candidates for the senior executive position. The system, licensed for more than 1,000 beds, includes comprehensive, full-service acute, skilled, rehabilitation, ambulatory care and behavioral health services for the community and West Coast. XYZ is dedicated to a public, quality-driven mission, and is embarking upon bold initiatives in preparing for its future through cost repositioning, partnerships with physicians and other providers and organizational transformation.

Qualified candidates must have at least 10 years of progressively responsible senior executive experience in health care with accountability for, and proven success in, medical staff relations, organizational development and leadership, cost management, and quality. Appropriate academic credentials, including a preference for post-graduate degree, and teaching hospital experience in aligning physician and institutional interests in managed care and developing the infrastructure for effectively competing in aggressive markets, are sought. Innovative management experience in broad-based work re-design and participative change management is essential. A commitment to the organization's public mission with public accountability, and experience in effective media relations and strong internal and external communications is required. XYZ is an equal opportunity employer.

The Board of Trustees will entertain resumes, through its consultant, until February 1. Please submit your resume by mail to: Board of Trustees, Search Committee.

CEO—Small Hospital

CHIEF EXECUTIVE OFFICER

County Community Hospital, a small hospital located in the beautiful mountains, is seeking a Chief Executive Officer to lead us into the 21st century.

This 25-bed hospital offers a range of in-patient and outpatient community services including Emergency, Outpatient Surgery, Physical Therapy and Cardiac Rehabilitation.

Candidates will have an in-depth knowledge of integrated health care delivery systems with the ability to drive a strategic plan as well as have a strong background in hospital financial and budgetary principles. A Bachelors degree and a minimum of 5 years experience in an administrative position within a hospital or health care setting are mandatory for this position. A Masters in Health Administration is preferred.

Competitive salary and benefit package complement the quality of lifestyle our rural location offers. If you are interested in this opportunity, please send a current resume or CV along with salary history to: Board of Trustees, Search Committee.

County Hospital is an equal opportunity employer and service provider.

COO

VICE PRESIDENT, OPERATIONS

XYZ Memorial Hospital is seeking a candidate for the position of Vice President. We are a strong and growing community hospital in an excellent location. The hospital is stable, well positioned, and offers comprehensive inpatient and outpatient services in an integrated network.

The successful candidate will have a MHA or equivalent degree and at least ten years of progressive experience demonstrating successful health care management skills. Please send resume to:

V.P. Human Resources
XYZ MEMORIAL HOSPITAL
PO Box

EOE

CFO

CHIEF FINANCIAL OFFICER

A 235 bed hospital in the Southeast has retained a firm to recruit for a new Chief Financial Officer. This position is a member of the executive team and has significant impact on the future shape of the organization. Candidates must have strong decision making abilities, good interpersonal skills, financial acumen and the ability to effectively interact with medical staff and board members.

Qualifications for this position include, a bachelor's degree, a CPA and master's is strongly preferred. Ideally, the individual will have experience and exposure to a managed care environment. This position offers an outstanding salary, benefits and relocation package. Please mail resumes in confidence or fax to: Board of Trustees, Search Committee.

COO

Chief Operating Officer

A well-respected and religiously-sponsored regional health-care system is seeking a Chief Operating Officer for a newly created position. Located in the Southwest this position reports to the System's Chief Executive Officer and is responsible for improving the competitive positioning of five operating units, reducing costs per adjusted discharge and enhancing services that complement other elements of this emerging, integrated delivery network.

The successful candidate will assume leadership and management of large-scale transformational processes, including re-engineering; implementation of a comprehensive information infrastructure; restructuring management systems and practices; and, the alignment of hospital services with community needs in a market that is moving quickly to managed care.

Qualified candidates must have: An MBA, MHA or related degree • 10+ years health care experience, with at least 3 years as an operations officer for a hospital or health system • Proven success at transforming hospital operations to effectively meet the challenges of managed care/capitation • Exceptional communication and interpersonal skills with the ability to effectively relate with individuals from a variety of ethnic and cultural backgrounds • Strong values and beliefs, coupled with integrity, creativity and a positive attitude.

An excellent compensation and benefits package, including a comprehensive relocation package, is provided. To respond, qualified candidates may submit their resumes in strictest confidence to: **Confidential Reply Service, P.O. Box 01.** An equal opportunity/affirmative action employer.

CNO

 ICE PRESIDENT
Nursing Service

We're seeking an individual who will bring vision and leadership to our full service community hospital.

At XYZ Hospital, you'll be a member of the Top Corporation, one of the leading systems of health care. As a member of Administration, you will be responsible to maintain and improve the delivery of efficient, cost-effective, quality care and patient services to the residents of coastal and surrounding communities.

As senior management, you will provide direction and leadership as you oversee operations of XYZ Hospital including development/management of plans of care, identify business development opportunities, oversee development of partnerships, maintain effective and efficient operation of Medical, Surgical, ICU, Surgery, Dialysis, Emergency, Mental Health, and Women's and Infants Center (140-beds), and ensure operational objectives remain consistent with the philosophy, mission, and strategic plan of XYZ Hospital and Top Corporation.

The candidate we seek will hold a degree in Nursing along with a Master's Degree in Business, Health care, or related field. Three to five years of progressive management experience to include all areas of hospital operations is required. Ability to work effectively with a diverse group of management, staff, and physicians is essential. In addition, proven skills in strategic planning, consensus building, CQI principles, and problem solving are necessary.

You will be compensated with a competitive salary and a flexible benefits package. For immediate consideration, please forward resume, with earnings history, to: **Director of Human Resources, XYZ Hospital.**

AA/EEO Employer

Coordinator, Quality Management

QUALITY MANAGEMENT COORDINATOR

XYZ Hospital seeks a self-directed individual to coordinate quality management functions including medical staff & hospitalwide QI, data collection/ evaluation & work injury mgt. 2 yrs hospital-based clinical experience (preferably in psych or PM&R) required; 1 yr UR/QI experience, PA licensed RN, and/or CPHQ preferred. We offer a generous compensation package & free parking! Fax a resume to HR or mail it to Human Resources.

Director, Patient Financial Services

DIRECTOR OF PATIENT FINANCIAL SERVICES

The position will report to the system VP Finance, and be responsible for 150 FTEs in credit, collections, billing and admissions. Preferred candidates will have 5+ years management experience in patient finance with a CPA/MBA preferred. Experience in effective management of multi-site operations is highly desired.

An extremely competitive compensation and relocation package is available.

Interested candidates should send a resume in confidence to: XYZ Hospital.

Director, MIS

DIRECTOR OF MANAGEMENT INFORMATION SYSTEMS

Responsibilities entail direct supervision and management of our Management Information Systems function. The requirements include strong interpersonal and organizational skills with management in a sophisticated information systems operation. A BS in Computer Science or related field required. A strong preference will be given to candidates with a Master's level education, HBOC or UNIX experience and/or experience in the development of integrated healthcare delivery systems.

Director, Marketing

HELP WANTED

MARKETING DIRECTOR

Located in the hills of a prominent New England hospital—a leader in chemical dependency treatment for adults and adolescents seeks aggressive Director of Marketing. Will be responsible for planning, organizing, leading and developing regional marketing/sales staff. Must have marketing management exp, background in managed care contracting and successful track record in sales. Competitive compensation program plus benefits. We offer a high quality of life and no state income or sales tax. Send resumes with cover letter to: Human Resources.

Director, Planning

Director of Planning

XYZ Health System, the second-largest healthcare delivery system in central U.S., is seeking a Director of Planning

XYZ Health System is comprised of: three hospitals (a 462-bed tertiary care center/teaching hospital, a 287-bed acute care hospital and a 194-bed community hospital); a primary care MSO/physician network, specialty PHO, ambulatory/primary care centers; home care, hospice and medical transportation services.

The Director of Planning will report to the VP of Planning and Marketing and will be responsible for strategic business planning activities for various business units throughout our growing delivery system. This position will work closely with peers in Strategic Planning, Market Research, Business Development and Regional Network Developments to develop action-oriented business plans and coordinate the development of new markets, products and services. Candidates must possess a masters degree in business or healthcare administration, marketing, social sciences or a related field and have 5 years experience in planning/business development in an integrated or regional healthcare system.

At XYZ Health System, we are devoted to the personal and professional growth of our Associates in an empowering, team-oriented and progressive environment. We offer a competitive compensation and benefits package. For consideration, please send your resume to: **The Medical Center: Attn: Human Resources.**

Director, Public Affairs

PUBLIC AFFAIRS DIRECTOR

XYZ Hospital, a leading Midwest Not-For-Profit Healthcare Organization, seeks an experienced, self-motivated professional with exceptional organizational and communication skills to:

Oversee Marketing/Public Relations Staff.
Direct Foundation's fund develop-. ment initiatives.
Manage five off-site family medicine practices.
Negotiate managed care contracts.
Develop Hospital Sponsored preferred provider product.

Position reports to the CEO and is a member of the six person executive leadership team. Candidate must possess MBA or MHA with five plus years experience preferred.

Excellent and comprehensive compensation and benefit package.

A brief statement of why you are best prepared to meet the rigors of this position will accompany the resume of the successful candidate.

Submit to: Director Human Resources

CLINICAL/QUALITY ASSURANCE

Rehabilitation

Director, Rehabilitative & Sub-Acute Services

XYZ Medical Center has a challenging opportunity for a professional with extensive experience managing the operations and clinical services of a Rehabilitative and Sub-Acute Services department.

The Director will be responsible for the development and implementation of business and division operation plans for our 30+ bed Acute Inpatient Rehabilitation Program, our 28 bed Sub-Acute Program, our Acute Therapy Rehabilitative Services and our Outpatient Rehabilitative Services. This will include overseeing the quality of service; expense control; effective management of capital and human resources; and participation in all strategizing for new building, construction/lease and unit renovation.

Exemplary candidates will have an entrepreneurial spirit, solid experience with CQI, and specialized knowledge of financial reimbursement and regulatory requirements specific to Rehabilitative and Sub-Acute Services (including knowledge of the Skilled Nursing Industry). Requires significant experience in operations management of Rehabilitative and Sub-Acute Services. Requires a Bachelor's degree in nursing, medical, or business specialty. Experience as a clinician providing Rehabilitative and Sub-Acute Services is helpful. Graduate degree, MBA/MHA/MS in hospital administration, healthcare administration or specialty field is a plus.

XYZ Medical Center offers an excellent compensation and benefits package. Please send resumes to: **Employee Relations; Attn: Job #1960023.** Principals Only. AA/EOE

XYZ MEDICAL CENTER

SUPPORT SERVICES

Purchasing

DIRECTOR OF PURCHASING

Enjoy living in an area with an easy going lifestyle, low crime rate, clean air and plenty of wide open space? XYZ Memorial Hospital, a progressive 76-bed hospital located in a year-round resort area, has a full-time opening for a Director of Purchasing. Bachelor's Degree or comparable experience. Sufficient previous experience in purchasing, receiving, distribution and stores. Healthcare experience preferred. Competitive salary and benefits. Deep Creek Lake and the Wisp Ski Resort are just a few of the many recreational offerings available. Interested applicants may send resume to: XYZ Memorial Hospital, Human Resources Department, 2 North Street, MD/EOE

Human Resources

Successful Southeastern Community Hospital Seeking
DIRECTOR OF HUMAN RESOURCES/
ASSISTANT ADMINISTRATOR

Rewarding position for an individual who is well organized and a self-starter. Requires Administrative Direction of Support Departments within the facility as well as all aspects of Personnel Management. Spanish, as first or second language, necessary. Salary compatible with blended duties.

For immediate consideration, please mail or fax resume to:

Office of Administration
Attention: Executive Secretary
General Hospital

Administrator

PSYCHIATRIC ADMINISTRATOR

The leading provider of inpatient and out-patient psychiatric services in south-central U.S. seeks an experienced administrator to direct and develop a comprehensive system of mental health care. The XYZ Center is a freestanding psychiatric hospital with office complex on-site, and several outpatient/outreach clinics throughout the region. Near Gulf Coast or Atlantic beaches. Interested candidates must have either MHA or MBA with experience in both inpatient and outpatient services administration, and should be committed to innovation, leadership, and market dominance. For immediate consideration, call or fax resume to.... Vice President, XYZ HEALTH SYSTEMS, INC.

INSURANCE MANAGED CARE

Administrator

HMO ADMINISTRATOR

Our client is a large National HMO with a strong financial foundation and commitment. We are seeking an individual with proven management skills in sales and operations, as well as some-one capable of building long term relationships with national accounts, brokers and consultants.

Please contact Management Resources

All Inquiries will be held in strict confidence.

Consultants

Manager

MANAGER OF MANAGED CARE

Since the 1900s XYZ Insurance Companies has been providing comprehensive, superior insurance protection and related services to select business owners, trade associations, and buying groups. Today, we are a highly respected, multiple-line company with $2.4 billion in assets, $804 million in premiums, and 2,600 employees. Our continued success and growth have prompted our search for an individual to direct the planning, development, and marketing of managed health care products and services that assist client policyholders in effectively managing cost and quality. This position is located in our Home Office in the Midwest.

Qualifications include:

- minimum 4 year college degree in business administration, marketing, health care management, or related field; and,

- minimum 5–7 years in managed care administration related work experience; and,

- excellent communication, organization, and negotiating skills.

We offer a professional work environment, comprehensive benefits program and a salary commensurate with education and experience. If interested, please send your RESUME and SALARY HISTORY to: **XYZ INSURANCE COMPANIES Attn: Human Resources.** An Equal Opportunity Employer M/F.

FEDERATED
INSURANCE

MANAGED HEALTHCARE

COO—Group Practice

HEALTHCARE

CHIEF OPERATING OFFICER Rapidly growing multi-site physician group practice in the northeast offers an immediate opportunity for a hands-on Chief Operating Officer. Reporting directly to the President/CEO, this professional must have a strong understanding of physician practices as well as a history of growing practice revenues. Experience in managed care risk contracts and knowledge of most current information systems required.

Our expanding organization offers an excellent compensation and benefits package. For immediate consideration, forward resume in confidence to: P.O. Box Address.

EOE m/f/d/v

Marketing

WE'VE GOT THE SOLUTION.
Healthcare Consultant

XYZ Solutions thru Technology (STT), a division of Top Corporation is experiencing rapid growth in the Southeast and has a variety of challenging coastal based opportunities.

➤ **PRACTICE LEADER/MANAGEMENT LEVEL**
Will act as Market Leader responsible for business development, strategic planning, implementation and delivery. Prior managed care, insurance, "Big 6" consulting, or software application development experience with a major software vendor a plus. Healthcare background required.

➤ **SR. or ASSOCIATE LEVEL CONSULTANT**
Must have strong background in client/server technologies and system implementation. Healthcare experience and market development capabilities a plus.

We offer a competitive salary and benefits package. For confidential consideration or more information, please send or fax resume to: **Staffing.**

MSO

PRESIDENT MSO

XYZ Inc., a fast growing health care industry leader based in the Southeast is seeking a highly motivated senior executive who has hands-on experience in managing a start-up HMO/PPO company. Qualified candidates must possess an advanced level degree—preferably health care related, a min. of 8+ years senior mgt. experience, and an in-depth knowledge of negotiating contracts for IPAs in several markets. Proven success with Physician Practice Mgt. is required. The ideal candidate should be able to manage and develop staff to take this division to a $250M revenue base and generate acceptable profit margins. Position reports to the Chief Operating Officer. Excellent relocation and benefit package available which includes stock options, 401(k), and insurance. V.P. Human Resources.

Director—Group Practice

XYZ
HEALTHCARE

MEDICAL GROUP
EXECUTIVE DIRECTOR

Successful, highly respected, multi-specialty medical group in California seeks Executive Director to lead organization into the next century. Qualifications include minimum of 10 years healthcare experience in an increasingly responsible management position; proven record of success in managing people in a complex, competitive environment; outstanding leadership and communication skills; and ability to attract and retain outstanding individuals to form a strong administrative team.

Successful candidate will assume overall responsibility for planning and administration of all non-clinical activities of the medical group. Reports directly to the Board of Directors and is ultimately responsible for the continued growth and success of the organization.

Top Medical Group, Inc. has served patients and businesses in the San Francisco Bay Area for over 40 years. With multiple locations in Silicon Valley between San Jose and San Francisco, its 160 physicians and 750 employees enjoy a wide range of recreational, cultural, and life-style opportunities. We offer an outstanding benefit and compensation package, with future increases linked directly to performance.

Interviews will be promptly scheduled for qualified candidates. For immediate consideration, please send resume in strictest confidence to: **Executive Search Committee Medical Group.**

EOE

Manager, Informatics

Manager, Data Services—Informatics

The selected applicant will define and implement data policies and strategies in support of Informatics and Disease Management Informatics strategic plan. This person will also define, implement and support the Informatics strategic database architecture and its associated environments, and participate in shaping company-wide data architecture. A BA/BS or relevant experience plus ten years' related work experience in data management and/or applications development required. Also must have a minimum of three years' experience in a supervisory/management role and large, multiple database (>200GB) management and design experience. Refer to Job Code 00.

ELDERLY SERVICES

Administrator

NURSING HOME ADMINISTRATOR

Seeking licensed NHA for 100 bed non-profit facility in Northeast area. This person must have minimum of 3 yrs. experience in LTC. BS or Masters degree. Must have excellent communication skills, be take charge person and have strong work ethic. Individual must be flexible, caring person who enjoys working with elderly and their families on daily basis. Send resume to: Executive Director.

CEO

EXECUTIVE DIRECTOR

XYZ Nurse Home Health Service, a leading Home Health Care Agency with approximately 240 employees, has an exceptional opportunity for an experienced Director.

Requirements include a Bachelor's Degree in Management, Business Administration, Nursing or other closely related field. A Master's Degree is helpful but not essential. Five years of progressive management responsibility in a service organization. Home Care or Health Care experience desirable.

This position requires leadership responsive to the changing needs of Health Care.

Send resume and salary requirements by October 15th to: **Director of Human Resources, XYZ NURSE HOME HEALTH SERVICE.**

EOE

A complete list of titles in our extensive *Opportunities* series

OPPORTUNITIES IN

Accounting
Acting
Advertising
Aerospace
Agriculture
Airline
Animal & Pet Care
Architecture
Automotive Service
Banking
Beauty Culture
Biological Science
Biotechnology
Broadcasting
Building Construction Trades
Business Communications
Business Management
Cable Television
CAD/CAM
Carpentry
Chemistry
Child Care
Chiropractic
Civil Engineering
Cleaning Service
Commercial Art & Graphic Design
Computer Maintenance
Computer Science
Computer Systems
Counseling & Development
Crafts
Culinary
Customer Service
Data & Word Processing
Dental Care
Desktop Publishing
Direct Marketing
Drafting
Electrical Trades
Electronics
Energy
Engineering
Engineering Technology
Environmental
Eye Care
Farming and Agriculture
Fashion
Fast Food
Federal Government
Film
Financial
Fire Protection Services

Fitness
Food Service
Foreign Language
Forestry
Franchising
Funeral Services
Gerontology & Aging Services
Health & Medical
Heating, Ventilation, Air Conditioning, and Refrigeration
High Tech
Home Economics
Homecare Services
Horticulture
Hospital Administration
Hotel & Motel
Human Resources Management
Information Systems
Installation & Repair
Insurance
Interior Design & Decorating
International Business
Journalism
Laser Technology
Law
Law Enforcement & Criminal Justice
Library & Information Science
Machine Trades
Marine & Maritime
Marketing
Masonry
Medical Imaging
Medical Sales
Medical Technology
Mental Health
Metalworking
Military
Modeling
Music
Nonprofit Organizations
Nursing
Nutrition
Occupational Therapy
Office Occupations
Optometry
Paralegal
Paramedical
Part-Time & Summer Jobs
Performing Arts
Petroleum
Pharmacy

Photography
Physical Therapy
Physician
Physician Assistant
Plastics
Plumbing & Pipe Fitting
Postal Service
Printing
Property Management
Psychology
Public Health
Public Relations
Publishing
Purchasing
Real Estate
Recreation & Leisure
Religious Service
Research & Development
Restaurant
Retailing
Robotics
Sales
Science Technician
Secretarial
Social Science
Social Work
Special Education
Speech-Language Pathology
Sports & Athletics
Sports Medicine
State & Local Government
Teaching
Teaching English to Speakers of Other Languages
Technical Writing & Communications
Telecommunications
Telemarketing
Television & Video
Theatrical Design & Production
Tool & Die
Training & Development
Transportation
Travel
Trucking
Veterinary Medicine
Visual Arts
Vocational & Technical
Warehousing
Waste Management
Welding
Writing
Your Own Service Business

VGM Career Horizons
a division of *NTC/Contemporary Publishing Company*
4255 West Touhy Avenue
Lincolnwood, Illinois 60646–1975